Let's Get It On!

"Real"istic Strategies for Winning the Sales Game

Scott Marker

This book is dedicated to my parents.

To my father, who helped with continual input, extensive reviewing and helped me become the person I am today.

To my mother, my biggest fan, who knew I could succeed at whatever I did.

Acknowledgments

I would like to thank all my friends, family and associates who have patiently listened to me talk about this book for over five years.

A big thank you to Carl Levi of PowerProof LLC and Lazaro Martinez for their meticulous editing and input, which polished my manuscript into the book it has become.

I appreciate the help of my wife in the final proofreading and her support over the years.

A special thanks to Shawn Gants for creating the great artwork and graphics in this book.

Thanks to Susan Reed of RoseCreative for the text typesetting and print preparation.

CONTENTS

CONTENTS (CONTINUED)

Foreword

You hold in your hands one of the most interesting and effective sales books you'll ever read.

At first glance, you may find the combination of Mixed Martial Arts and selling an odd choice. However, as you read further you'll realize that this may in fact be the best combination of sales effectiveness ideas ever put together.

Selling is a highly technical process and one that is always won by the superior salesperson. The challenge for many sales organizations over the years is that they didn't know what worked. What replicable skills should be taught, honed and tested? The same question was asked over and over again in the martial arts. The questions were often answered with great speculation but without test in actual combat, much like many of the "sales techniques" and "sales processes." In the martial arts a test is devised, matches two men of equal skill, armed with their techniques of choice and allows them to fight with minimal rules of engagement. Very quickly, an effective style emerged. As it turned out, it wasn't boxing, wrestling, kung fu, judo or karate that was best. No single art could be demonstrated to be the best alone. The fighters who won consistently adapted their styles and added the effective techniques of other styles and the Mixed Martial Arts, MMA, phenomenon was born.

In selling, a very similar war is being waged every day. Traditional sales systems and techniques are falling by the wayside as consumers become more and more educated. They understand the processes you use to influence and persuade them to buy and they develop effective defenses against traditional systems. And that is where the Mixed Selling Arts emerge.

Scott Marker has a unique background. He's been a top producer in every organization he's ever worked in. He's also been a winning mixed martial artist. And, while he has perfected a number of skills in each undertaking, what makes him successful is his skill in breaking down techniques, assimilating the core components of each and then practicing and applying them until they are perfect. But what makes them effective for you is his ability to teach them in a fast to learn process. Scott has purified sales effectiveness by leveraging the business and martial strategy to create a selling system effective enough for today's most complex sale and solid enough to weather the test of time. And, he's proven it over and over again in multiple industries and sales opportunities.

Let's Get It On! walks you through not only the most crucial skill sets you must learn to sell more than you've ever sold before, but also through the critical mindsets that allow you to master these techniques and become a champion in sales or any other skill you choose to master.

Scott has a completely unique way of drawing corollaries between mixed martial arts strategy and sales strategy. The reason it works is because of his focus on strategy, not on applying technique after technique just because you can or to show you know them.

Sales techniques that can be easily learned and parroted are easily defeated. If you learn the puppy dog close, the drop, the take away, the T or any other techniques and try and apply them, your client or their purchasing agents have already developed a technique to counter you. Information has leveled the playing field. What works is strategically combined, tightly focused sales efforts that leverage time tested skills with new hyper-effective skills that allow you to go head to head with the competition and walk away with the order.

The martial arts are all about strategy, one action sets up another. The master isn't the person who practices 2000 techniques but who practices one technique 2000 times. They practice the skill again and again in every possible combination, in every possible condition, against every possible opponent.

There is a saying in martial arts that says the more they sweat in the dojo the less they bleed in the ring. The more your team trains in the backroom the more they make in the boardroom.

The advent of the internet changed selling forever but sales training never caught up, until now.

Let's Get It On! takes the best of traditional sales skills, updates them for today and combines them with cutting edge modern tactics and strategy: tested, proven and ready for you to learn.

If you are serious about selling and want to take yourself or your team to the new level, you need the information Scott has thoroughly detailed in this book.

If ever in the history of selling there was an absolute requirement for a new approach, this is it.

Now, turn the page and *Let's Get It On!*

Dave Lakhani

Author: *Persuasion: The Art of Getting What You Want* and *Subliminal Persuasion: Influence and Marketing Secrets they Don't Want You To Know*
Boise, ID

Introduction

Sales and the Mixed Martial Arts Revolution

**What had been taught for decades
had failed in a true test.**

For decades, martial artists argued about whose system or style was the best. Then in 1993, with the advent of the Ultimate Fighting Championship (UFC), all the theories and concepts could be tested under realistic conditions. There were very limited rules: no biting, no poking eyes, no hitting or grabbing the groin and <u>no gloves</u>. This was going to be the ultimate test to prove which system, or style of martial arts, was the best.

The first Ultimate Fighting Championship (UFC) pitted several styles of martial arts against each other: kickboxing, Sumo, karate, Shootfighting, boxing and Brazilian Jiu-Jitsu. For years there had been much talk about what worked best in actual street altercations. The UFC was as close as you could get to the real thing. The fights would be held in a large octagon cage and were originally called "no holds barred" (NHB) competitions.

Most of the competitors had earned black belts in their discipline of martial arts, and video clips showed many of the competitors training before they got into the cage. What became immediately apparent was that most, if not all, of the teachings in their schools were not effective when they started to fight in the cage.

Only one fighter performed the same as his training previewed. He was Royce Gracie, with Brazilian Jiu-Jitsu. The Ultimate Fighting Championship (UFC) proved that some systems were better prepared than others for a realistic fight. More importantly, many of the systems' techniques did not work well when put to the test.

Because of UFC, the martial arts world would be forever changed and the mixed martial arts revolution had begun.

The term mixed martial arts "MMA" has replaced the original titles of the events that previously were called "no holds barred" or NHB. NHB events were to prove the superiority of a particular discipline that usually specialized in one particular range, i.e., kicking, punching or grappling. As these types of events have become mainstream and have more rules, they have started to be recognized as legitimate sporting events. The term "mixed" came about because over the years all the competitors have had to evolve by mixing the best techniques from many different systems in order to be well rounded. MMA has become a hybrid of systems.

In today's sales environment, many companies comfortably promote the belief that their methods for approaching prospects and acquiring customers work very well. Unfortunately, too many of these same companies get left behind in the real world of intense competition.

Many have given credit to Bruce Lee, a famous martial arts expert and movie star in the early 1970's, for envisioning the mixed martial arts. He saw a future where any martial artist would need an understanding of all the ranges of combat. He or she would have to take the best from each system that specializes in each range and disregard anything that would not work under realistic conditions. In order to compete successfully in today's level of competition, fighters have to understand all the ranges: kicking, punching, clinching/takedowns and ground grappling. Similarly, today's *sales professionals* must have a thorough understanding of all aspects of the sales cycle.

Since 1993, there has been more advancement in the martial arts than in the previous 200 years. How could that be, you ask? There are several reasons, but it took the Ultimate Fighting Championship to shock the martial arts world into facing the fact that much of what was being taught was not realistic. For years before the UFC, the majority of the martial arts world "Couldn't handle the truth!"

I wrote an article entitled "Combat Effective" in 1994 for my Kenpo Karate association, Kenpo 2000, which stressed my concern that much of the material taught in the martial arts schools, including ours, was not suited for real world street altercations.

Here is an excerpt of that article:

> *"The truth was that many martial arts systems stressed modern, up-to-date techniques with sound concepts and principles, but combatants would never be able to apply the step-by-step ritualistic techniques in real life situations. Like a lot of martial artists, they are on the right track with valid concepts, but the physical mechanics are too far removed from the real street environment."*

In order to be combat effective, we have to make sure our techniques work in the school and in the street. Don't just keep adding moves to a technique but try to make each move more and more effective. A few moves that work are far better than a group of moves that look fancy but would never work in the street. We owe it to our students to make sure what we teach them is for real. As Skip Hancock says in his book, 'We need students who are confident, and most important, competent'."

I have found the same situation to be true with much of the sales training given by all the companies I have worked for. The information provided was unrealistic and impractical outside of the classroom.

Long before I began a successful career in sales, I became involved in the martial arts. I was awarded my first black belt from the International Kenpo Karate association in 1991 and I received a fifth degree black belt from the Kenpo 2000 association in 2007 by Professor Skip Hancock. Also, I was awarded a blue belt by Rickson Gracie American Jiu-Jitsu association by my instructor Professor Pedro Sauer in 1997. Over the years, I have competed in many local and international karate tournaments, winning numerous trophies. One trophy I am most proud of is when I competed and won my match in the first official mixed martial arts (MMA) tournament in Boise, Idaho in 1996. These days, I don't compete in tournaments, but I still train and teach the martial arts, and I am the Head of Officials for MMA, Idaho Athletic Commission.

I have taught numerous martial arts seminars to students from all over the United States and from many other countries. A fellow instructor and I have taught rape prevention classes for the Idaho State Department of Finance and Department of Commerce.

Looking back at my martial arts experiences, I have been very fortunate; and people have been tolerant of my outspoken views, rebellion and ideas that went against the status quo. Professor Skip Hancock, my Kenpo instructor, and other fellow instructors put up with my outspoken views for years. A fellow instructor at our school and I were awarded the first Ed Parker Award from the Kenpo 2000 association for our contributions to the continued evolution of the marital arts over the years. This was inscribed on the plaque:

"For your contributions to Kenpo, the Art that we love. The indomitable spirit of Ed Parker, the Father of our Art, abides within you. Always training, experimenting, analyzing, revising, and devising to contribute to the evolution of Kenpo. Like Ed

Parker, you continually search for what is practical for each time and place. And like Ed Parker, you freely share your knowledge with both young and old. You are a model to all of our students. You continually do the Art, simply because you love it!"

Just as the UFC forced the martial arts world to face the truth, this book offers tested concepts to companies and managers to help them significantly improve their sales.

The *truths* presented here will help *sales professionals* improve their closure rates, and the ideas presented will yield success, even when working for a company that is unwilling to change and "Can't handle the truth!" The reader will notice that I have coined certain words and phrases relative to selling. They are in *italics* in the text and can be found in the glossary. Also, while writing this book, I have read numerous studies concerning sales. For expedience, I have listed all of them in the reference list at the end of this book.

I have learned from my years of marital arts training that "discipline" is a key success. I have since found that is a key to success in the sales.

Success is never a perfect science, but I am always striving to "increase my odds," whether in closing a sale or in winning a competitive match.

Since retaining good customers and closing more sales is the acknowledged goal, **let's get it on!**

1

Beneficial Parallels Between Sales & The Martial Arts

Selling arts and the martial arts

I have learned many things from my martial arts training over the past 25 plus years, and I have discovered that there are numerous beneficial parallels between the martial arts and the *selling arts*, which lead me to create the "*mixed selling arts*." Many of the lessons from the martial arts can substantially help companies, sales managers and *sales professionals* who are interested in improving their sales strategies and techniques. Much of the innovative thinking from the martial arts world can make a direct and beneficial impact on companies' sales.

Senior Grandmaster Ed Parker was famous for using stories, analogies and metaphors to improve the teaching of his ideas, techniques and system of martial arts. Accordingly, I learned the power of using stories, analogies and metaphors to help teach martial arts and the MSA - mixed selling arts.

You have to understand your *base* in both *selling arts* and the martial arts. In the martial arts today, you have to have an understanding of all the ranges of combat to build a solid *base*, which is your foundation.

Strategic Combat Cycle (SCC) breakdown:

Out of range - Is where you cannot strike or be struck without a major foot maneuver.

Contact range - Allows you to strike or be struck by long distance weapons (i.e. kicks.)

Contact Penetration range - Is that distance where you can strike or be struck by the fist, knees and elbows.

Contact Manipulation range - Occurs when you are starting to make body contact and have close-in fighting and grappling from a standing position. This includes clinching, striking with fists, knees, elbows and takedowns.

Ground Manipulation range - Is where you hit the ground, utilizing grappling arts (i.e. Brazilian Jiu-Jitsu, Judo and wrestling) while inserting strikes, chokes and locks.

These ranges can and do overlap, but they have to be viewed separately to be better understood and improved upon in each range of combat.

In the sales world, there are also different stages of engagement. Each stage is very broad and must be broken down to be fully understood. One needs to have an understanding of his *base* of sales in order to create a solid sales foundation. To better understand and improve an organization's sales, it is first necessary to view sales from an all-encompassing perspective.

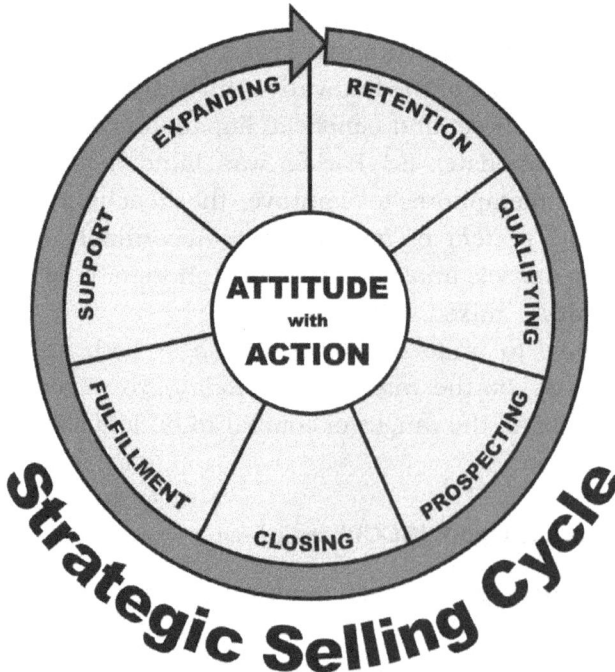

Strategic Selling Cycle

EXPANDING · RETENTION · QUALIFYING · PROSPECTING · CLOSING · FULFILLMENT · SUPPORT

ATTITUDE with ACTION

The following is my breakdown, which I have named the **Strategic Selling Cycle (SSC)**:

Every stage of the **Strategic Selling Cycle** contains a form of the word strategy for a reason. This is to reinforce continually the fact that companies always have to plan before any action is taken.

> **KEY TAKEAWAY:**
> **"Remember that having no plan is still a plan."**
> **Walt Davis, manager, sales professional**

Strategic planning should incorporate elements that will help you meet your goal. I believe that strategizing is the art of carefully planning towards a specific goal. Many companies and sales forces go blindly forward and sometimes they have a measure of success. However, if they have a strategic game plan, they can increase their chances of long-term continued success.

Attitude with ACTION! Attitude is at the center of the **Strategic Selling Cycle**, because attitude and passion are the key ingredients that drive a *sales professional* to get up after being knocked down. Trying again after a setback and taking a "no" as a "not now", are keys to sales success. Attitude is like your body; it needs to be exercised positively to continue to be strong. However, great intentions and a positive attitude are not enough. The key is to combine them with **ACTION**.

Retention Strategy stage - Is when you are implementing strategies and techniques to retain profitable and beneficial customers.
Examples are special pricing, incentives, reward programs, dedicated account representatives, gifts, etc.
(Retention is widely agreed upon to be key to a company's profitability and success, but it is the most misunderstood and forgotten stage. That is why I list it first on the "Strategic Selling Cycle.")

Qualifying Strategy stage - Here, you are trying to identify specific customers who would be a good fit for your products and services. What is a prospect's potential? Just as important, is the prospect a fit for you and your company? Not all prospects are a fit for your company. The first step in this stage is to evaluate and eliminate weak opportunities and to pursue only prospects that have a true potential. Qualifying continues into the Prospecting Strategy stage. You are ensuring that the particular prospect or customer offers a profitable opportunity.

Prospecting Strategy stage - You will now start determining strategies for the first engagement with a prospective customer. Many companies equate this stage to cold calling. Cold calling is a part of this stage. It also includes *warm calling* which is where the prospect somehow knows of you or is referred to you. One of your immediate goals is to get an appointment. An in-person appointment is typically the best, but a web meeting, email or phone call can be a good option. Once you get the appointment, you start to investigate to qualify whether the customer is a fit for your company. The *Qualifying stage* somewhat overlaps into this stage. Similarly, in the martial arts, kicking and punching can overlap but have to be separated out to be better understood.

Closing Strategy stage - You are trying to convince or persuade the customer to buy your products and services. This can be done on the first meeting, or in multiple meetings, or through tools (i.e. proposals.) The ultimate goal is to close the deal, or better yet, to confirm an agreement to a partnership, which will lead to multiple closed deals. In any long-term partnership, you are constantly closing by reminding the customer why they should continue to buy from you and your company.

Fulfillment Strategy stage - At this point, your company provides the product and services that you and your customer agreed upon your *promise* or obligation. An example could be new network printers, delivered and installed at a specified, agreed upon date, for a specified price.

Support Strategy stage - Now, your customer receives backing and assistance for your company's products and services. This can mean helping customers with new, existing or previous orders. Example: A printer company giving telephone or online help/customer support for printer problems, order status or updates.

Expanding Strategy stage - Once you have a customer, you should continually seek ways to sell more of the same products and services, as well as any new products and services your company offers. For instance, a car company that sells lease and service *programs* to businesses and then gets a new agreement not only to lease cars to a particular company, but also to service their fleet. Another example is a business that sells a line of shampoos and convinces an existing customer to stock several new container sizes.

The **Strategic Selling Cycle** is an essential tool used to better understand sales. It is your base; the foundation of your sales force. It reminds us that, in sales, we are strategizing and selling constantly. It is a never-ending cycle that continually flows from one stage to another. As in the martial arts world, one can spend a lifetime on one particular range (i.e. kicking range), but in today's world of MMA - mixed martial arts competitors need to have a solid understanding of each range to be a complete fighter. The same applies to MSA - mixed selling arts. One may spend a lifetime studying and perfecting closing; but, if you rarely get in the door, your success as a sales professional will be substantially reduced. Companies and sales forces can specialize in one stage or stages, but they must have the strong foundation of all the stages to be the most successful.

Any company wanting to win business in today's ultra-competitive world must have a solid understanding of all the stages in the sales process. Just as in the mixed martial arts, you have to understand and learn each range and how each is *connected* to the next. In the mixed selling arts, both the company and the sales force must learn how each of the stages is *connected*.

Mario Sperry, MMA, Brazilian Jiu-Jitsu former champion and expert instructor, states on his training DVD's, "All the moves and techniques I show you are connected." This is a very important point for success in sales. The strategies, ideas and techniques I explain are often used in combination in many areas and are *connected*.

Connecting of Ideas

Another important concept I will use throughout this book is the *threading* of ideas. I recommend companies, sales managers and the *sales professional* use *threading* to help maximize the learning of new ideas.

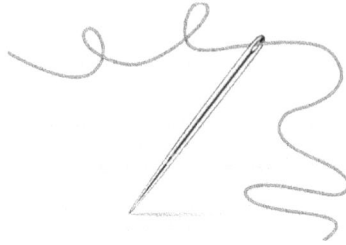

Threading of Ideas

Threading refers to applying a proven strategy, idea or technique in one area of sales or the martial arts to another area. Those tactics proven to be effective in the **Prospecting stage** can be used successfully in the **Expansion stage**. The *Connecting* of ideas refers to two or more strategies, ideas or techniques building on each other.

Ideas will be utilized in one stage of the **SSC** and then again, either with *threading* and/or in combination. Moreover, stages need to be *connected*, to build and enhance each other.

KEY TAKEAWAY

The ultimate success for both the company and the sales force is to have a solid foundation in the understanding of the cycle of sales.

Do not be fooled. Many companies and *sales professionals* are going to think that they know all about the sales cycle stages. Be careful. You might know some of the *"revenue-generating activities"*, but you can gain a better understanding and be introduced to new ideas that will help you become much more successful in sales.

An instructor from a martial arts school made an interesting comment, which came after a class that I taught on a submission hold. I had taught the particular technique before and the basic technique has been around for hundreds of years. He told me that he teaches the technique to some students who are in law enforcement and he thought there was no possible way to make the submission technique any tighter, safer and more effective until after my class. Remember, the same applies in sales, it is not always the techniques that are different but the refinements and the way you apply them that are new.

KEY TAKEAWAY

It is not always the techniques that are different but the refinements and the way you apply them that are new.

The **Strategic Selling Cycle** is a great tool to improve sales. Similarly, in the mixed martial arts world, a great way to help a competitor improve his overall game is by breaking down his skills to each belt level in each of the fighting ranges. He might be at a black belt level at kicking and punching but at a white belt, beginner level in grappling on the ground. It is important to break down a fighter's and salesperson's game and look for places to improve. This great idea I originally heard on a grappling DVD by Erik Paulson, former MMA champion, top MMA coach and trainer. This idea was easy then to apply to the sales world.

In the MSA - *mixed selling arts*, you or your sales force might be at a black belt level in prospecting but at a brown belt, intermediate, level at closing and at a white belt level at retention.

Use this concept to analyze the strengths and weaknesses of your game, whether in the martial arts or the sales world.

In the sales world, many of the *basics* have been known for decades, but the refinements are new and are continually changing and improving. The key in sales and the martial arts is *sophisticated basics,* not complicated basics. As John Sculley, former CEO of Apple, is famous for being quoted, "I think more and more people are learning that you have to simplify, not complicate. Simplicity is the ultimate sophistication." This line of thinking is another *Universal Truth,* borrowed from another famous person from long ago.

KEY TAKEAWAY

"Simplicity is the ultimate sophistication."
Leonardo da Vinci, (April 15, 1452 – May 2, 1519),
painter, scientist, engineer, mathematician, writer,
and inventor

2

MMA & MSA Methodologies

Bruce Lee was right

Take the best and disregard the rest

Develop a framework & base

Continual learning and improvements

I have already mentioned that the late, great martial artist Bruce Lee's thinking was ahead of his time. He would strive to take moves and ideas from the best of the martial art systems and then add them to his base system of self-defense. He named his art Jeet Kune Do (JKD). There is still much discussion and disagreement regarding whether he had a style, a system or just a concept. I will follow his advice and take what is useful to "me" and utilize his ideas to help improve both my martial arts and sales methodologies.

Bruce Lee has been quoted numerous times saying, "Take what is useful and reject what is useless." His ideas have proven to be true with the advent of the mixed martial arts (MMA). He spoke often of *Truths* and *The Truth* in his teachings. To be considered a *Truth* means that a technique or move has been proven in actual combat, or realistic competition. He also said that no one system or style has all the answers to every situation. Therefore, no system or type of martial arts was the holder of *The Truth*. Consequently, nobody has all the answers in every situation. This belief constantly reinforces the need to make adjustments and to improve.

The mixed martial arts (MMA) have proven this to be true. In the early years of the Ultimate Fighting Championship competition, Brazilian Jiu-Jitsu seemed to be *The Truth*. Over and over again, practitioners of Brazilian Jiu-Jitsu were victorious over all other systems of martial arts. But as the years went on, many *Truths* were discovered. Wrestling, Muay Thai-kickboxing and Brazilian Jiu-Jitsu all were shown to be *Truths*, meaning that all were proven to work under pressure in actual competition, not just in school theory. At the same time, all the martial arts systems with "exotic" bases and techniques have vanished from MMA competitions.

As long as the competitors knew the *Universal Truths* of all the ranges: kicking, punching, kneeing, clinching/takedowns, and ground grappling, they would have a probability of winning.

> *Universal Truths* = **Strategies and ideas that have worked <u>repeatedly</u>, under realistic conditions, for <u>numerous people</u>, and have been found to have a high probability of success over time.**

During my 20 years in seven different industries of business-to-business (B2B) sales, I searched for new ideas and for *Universal Truths* in all the different stages of sales. I have followed the mixed martial arts (MMA) model of building a *base* of *Universal Truths* and then continually improving and refining the *basics*. This search has developed into my *MSA - mixed selling arts methodology*:

> *A field of continual study of sales methods built around a base of Universal Truths. Striving to constantly improve and sophisticate the basics. Ultimately, it is a way of making learning and improving a way of life.*

You want to build a *base* of *Universal Truths*. Then, it is easier continually to improve and refine the *basics*. Remember though, don't add untested strategies and techniques. It is necessary to test several times under realistic conditions before adding to your *base*.

I have found that in the MSA - *mixed selling arts* and in the martial arts, a good *base* built on *Universal Truths* is like the solid foundation on which to build a house. It is easy to add new and to refine existing strategies and techniques to a good, strong, realistic *base*. During my research for this book, I found that sales experts had written articles after I had already written a section for this book; and, although we used a few different words, the similarities were amazing. This situation just reinforces the fact that there are many *Universal Truths*.

A lot of the ideas out there today are good, but a *sales professional* with no *base* will not be able to apply new ideas efficiently or to improve as fast. Many sales and martial arts experts will argue that there is no superior sales program or martial art. They believe that it is the superior individual who is the only key. This is a half-truth. It is accurate that some individuals are just naturally gifted; but, by having a great system built of *Universal Truths,* a good individual will become great and a great individual will become a superstar. Don't be fooled, some sales systems are superior to others.

As mentioned before, in the first couple years of Ultimate Fighting Championship competitions, many of the styles looked totally different on their training video clips before the competition. They had exotic *bases* and moves that you never saw in competition. They looked good in the school or demonstrations but failed in a realistic test.

Mixed martial arts competitors are now mixing many styles together. The grappling range, for example, has mixed Brazilian Jiu-Jitsu, wrestling, Sambo and Judo. In a little over a decade of competition, ninety percent of the competitors look fairly similar when they compete. Some favor certain aspects, such as striking or grappling; but, to a new fan or spectator, they look nearly alike in what they do. If there is much difference at all, it is because of the individual's physical makeup.

Companies need to build a *base* of *Universal Truths*, along with *basics* that are *Truths* and *Universal Truths*. Retention, Qualifying, Prospecting, Closing, Fulfillment, Support and Expanding stages have been proven to be a sound framework. If a company builds its *base* with exotic, unrealistic ideas for the real world, the sales force will be less efficient and easier for the competition to beat.

I was reading an article by a top sales expert and I respect him very much. He said that at every presentation he makes to a *sales professional* audience, he asks for a show of hands of those who had learned a sales system. Most in the audience would raise their hands. Then he would ask them to keep their hands up if they use that system on every sales call. Every hand would go down. When he would ask the audience why that was, he would get many answers.

11

"Too cumbersome," "too pushy," answers with the same theme. They were unrealistic for the real world. The sales expert then went on to say that he is against selling systems and that the focus should be on the customer, not a system. That's true. Focusing on the customer IS a top priority, but to improve in anything, there has to be a solid *base* that includes workable and realistic systems.

Why are so many people against a *base* including sales systems? As I stated before, a lot of the information is not founded on *Universal Truths*. It is not practical outside of the sales training classroom. As a result, many *sales professionals* get frustrated and just wing it. They might do well, but if they have a solid, realistic *base* and *basics* they will do even better. Recent large studies back up what I have known for years. Companies that follow a proven sales methodology and process continually outperform companies with sales forces that do not.

In the mixed martial arts (MMA), there are a number of similar attacks to defend against. Certain types of punches, kicks and takedowns become common after awhile.

Similarly, in many sales situations, there are some predictable happenings. In the **Closing Stage** for example, you will get similar objections: "it costs too much" or "I have no funds" and "we will get back to you." A *sales professional* trained in a realistic system will be armed with strategies and techniques that will help in dealing with and overcoming these common objections.

One of the aims of writing this book is the same as the goal of every martial arts seminar that I teach. I refine and sophisticate the *basics* and tools that can be added to anyone's *base*. Material then can be taken from my class and used in competition or in a street altercation with just a little bit of practice. If the participant already has a solid *base*, it is even easier for him/her to understand and learn.

Companies need to build a sales framework, or fundamental structure. It is a high level view of the company's sales structure that includes a sales methodology with a *base* and terminology to expedite learning. Companies need to have an organized structure for their sales force and/or sales department. The following diagram illustrates the *MSA* framework.

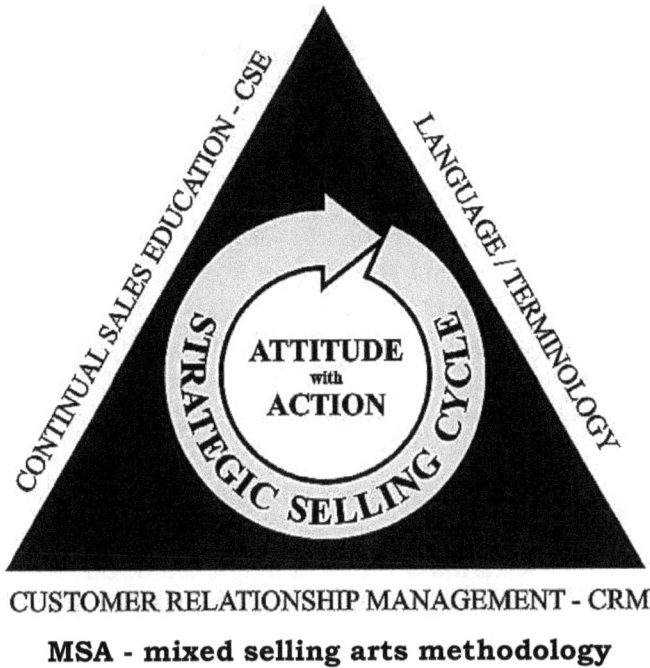

CUSTOMER RELATIONSHIP MANAGEMENT - CRM

MSA - mixed selling arts methodology

The *mixed selling arts methodology* is represented by a triangle with terminology on the right side, *Customer Relationship Management - CRM* on the bottom and *Continued Sales Education - CSE* on the left side. There is a circle in the middle representing the **Strategy Selling Cycle** and Attitude with Action in the middle.

This model will help sales organizations to better understand and ultimately improve sales results. Understanding a company's sales structure will help in understanding sales in its entirety, not just as an isolated piece. By understanding the entire "game", sales forces and companies will be substantially more effective at each "play".

All levels in the organization, from the CEO down, need to understand the sales methodologies and the sales framework. Studies are confirming what I have known for years. Companies have to have a sales structure, methodology. It should comprise technology, systems, best practices, processes and a sales language. These all become part of the company's culture. In all sales meetings, anything relating to sales, the message, methods and sales terminology has to be used constantly and consistently to be reinforced.

The **Strategic Selling Cycle** is the *base* of your sales process. How you and your company execute its Retention, Qualifying, Prospecting, Closing, Fulfillment, Support and Expanding strategies will be done

13

in *your own unique style*. Once you understand the overall sales framework, such as the MSA methodology, and have a *base*, such as the **Strategic Selling Cycle**, it is much easier to make improvements and continually add new ideas.

Part of any sales organization's culture should be continually to seek new ideas and improvements. The mixed martial arts (MMA) way of thinking is <u>revolutionary</u>. It has become its own methodology. The martial arts world has seen more change and improvement in the past decade than in the previous two centuries. This is because in the MMA, fighters are in a constant state of refinement and improvement. They are learning new ideas from all over the world to improve their *base*, themselves, their coaches and their fighting teams. It is part of the culture and a way of life.

In the business world, the search for new ideas and improvements often is called innovation. Many times the innovations are attributed to collaboration. These terms are talked about often, but with mediocre success at best. In professions such as engineering, law or medicine, continued education is required. In the medical world, professionals have to have a certain amount of CME - Continued Medical Education credits to maintain their licenses or certifications. In the sales world, there needs to be Continued Sales Education requirements for all sales forces.

In the mixed martial arts world, continued learning and innovation is looked at as fun and just part of the challenge. It is a positive mindset, not a negative. In the MMA world, innovation is happening at a rapid pace and can be a daily or weekly event. How can this be? It's a different mentality. Learning is half the fun. However, there is a "but". Something is accepted as an innovation only after it has been tested several times and found to be successful in a realistic environment. Then and only then is it considered to be a new innovation.

Things always change.... Not really

Companies' top executives, sales managers and sales forces have to look at continued learning, collaboration and innovation as fun and part of the game. I often hear people say, "Everything always changes," and it's said in a negative light. The mindset is that they constantly have to start from scratch.

By following the MSA methodology you never have to start from scratch. Let me use a football analogy. Our local college football team, Boise State Broncos, is down by seven points at halftime. In the locker room, the coach tells the team they need to make some adjustments. He says something like, "They are beating us on the...." The players don't roll around on the ground and start complaining that everything always changes. No, this type of talk is just part of the game and 80% percent of the game never changes. They always play on a one hundred-yard field, with four downs and field goals. It never changes. With this mindset, being told to consider the coach's analysis isn't so overwhelming. Environmental changes, natural turf vs. artificial turf, and outdoor vs. indoor fields are examples of the 20% that will require adjustments and refinements. These types of changes have always been part of the game and a part that makes it fun. The same applies to the sales world. Eighty percent of the sales process never really changes. Retention, qualifying, prospecting, closing, supporting and expanding existing business haven't and don't change.

With a solid base like the **Strategic Selling Cycle** or any other *base* built on *Truths* and *Universal Truths*, eighty percent does <u>not</u> always change. You are not reinventing the wheel, but you are continually making refinements, adjustments and new innovations.

The Audio-Tech Business Book Summaries' February 2006 edition talks about the 1980's book "In Search of Excellence." It highlighted several companies that were having outstanding performance results. By the 1990's, many of them were not top performers and some were struggling. They may have had a solid *base* but obviously had not made adjustments and refinements as the environment changed. To remain competitive, you must have a solid *base* and a methodology for constant improvement and learning.

Royce Gracie, winner of the first several UFC - Ultimate Fighting Championships, was found in 1993 to have a system that was a *Universal Truth*, realistic grappling. A little over a decade later, just knowing Brazilian Jiu-Jitsu doesn't guarantee victory. What happened? The environment changed. All the competitors now know Brazilian Jiu-Jitsu to different degrees and how to defend against it. Fighters are now well-rounded in all the ranges of combat: kicking, punching, clinching / takedowns and ground grappling. Today's competitors' *bases* include all the ranges and the *Truths* that have been discovered in realistic environments.

KEY TAKEAWAY

In order for a company and its employees to continually improve, they have to love to learn!

15

In the MSA world, strategies and techniques performed exactly the same, month after month, might not work after a while, because the environment has changed. Sometimes, though, the strategies and techniques might look the same to an outside observer; but, on closer observation, there have been subtle refinements that make them continue to be effective. There is no place where this is more evident than in prospecting for new business. Many sales organizations know "what" to do, prospect for new business, but do not know "how" to do it the most effective way. Prospecting for new business has been going on nearly forever, but many of the refinements and improvements are new. Prospecting, closing and retention are not the keys to success. How you prospect, close and retain business is the first key. But even fewer companies know "why" a certain way is the most effective.

KEY TAKEAWAY

Many companies know WHAT to do but do not know HOW to do it the most effective way. And even fewer know WHY a certain way is most effective.

The MSA - *mixed selling arts model* needs to be part of a company's sales methodology, inspiring people to love to learn. One important key distinction is to make sure you don't create a bunch of *Bone Buriers*.

Bone Buriers are a classic problem in the martial arts world. Students and instructors love to learn new techniques but never internalize the new material. They just keep on learning one new move after another. Then, they can say, "I learned that move." The martial artist ends up learning and memorizing numerous techniques that could never be utilized in a realistic situation. A story that was told to me illustrates this problem:

There was a master and his dog traveling through the desert. The master would give his dog a nice juicy bone, only to have the dog go bury the bone and run back to the master. This happened over and over again. When they had traveled to the middle of the desert, the dog became hungry and the master didn't have any more bones. The dog hunted and hunted but could not remember where he had buried any of his bones.

To improve, you have to utilize, apply and internalize the new knowledge.

In one of the early Ultimate Fighting Championship events, I saw a new leg lock used by one of the fighters who eventually won the event. That was on a Friday and on Monday, sparring night, I used the exact leg lock in class and tapped my opponent out; made him give up. Remember, the key is not to only learn new ideas, but also to apply the knowledge quickly.

> **KEY TAKEAWAY**
> **Don't be a "Bone Burier"...**
> **Internalize, don't just memorize!**

The great Jack Welch, former CEO of General Electric, was known to tell his top executives and managers always to look for new ideas and that a portion of those ideas will come from outside of the company. He created a culture of always looking for fresh ideas, acquiring good ideas from anywhere and then putting them into action quickly. What Mr. Welsh may not have known is that his thinking was in line with Bruce Lee's and now the entire MMA world.

When I am training in the martial arts and an opponent has given me a particularly tough time during a match, I think about what I could have done better. I ask for help from fellow instructors in order to make adjustments to overcome the challenges in my next match against that opponent. Making adjustments and refinements during a match and after a match is part of continual improvement. These tactics also help me in future matches against other opponents. Again, the mindset is positive, competitive, and I consider it fun to figure out how to overcome the challenge in future matches. All the students and fellow instructors in our martial arts school have the same "passion" for learning, improving and innovating.

In the sales world, this process of reflecting after a sales call is a *post-call* meeting. I believe this type of positive mindset is missing for many sales forces today.

A positive mindset is a key ingredient for constant improvement in developing more sales.

> **KEY TAKEAWAY**
> **"An organization's ability to learn and translate that learning into action rapidly is the ultimate competitive business advantage."**
> Jack Welch, Former General Electric chairman and CEO

I was in the weight room one day when a couple of young men

who follow the MMA competition asked me if I was still teaching. I told them, "Of course. I am still teaching, rolling around and learning." They both said, "Still learning? You have been training for years. You are an instructor. You don't still take lessons?" I replied, "Yes, I am still learning. It is a never-ending quest. There is always something new to learn and that is half the fun!" They both looked puzzled. Many people think that you know it all just because you have been in the martial arts for a long time or because you are a black belt. How wrong they were and are!

In the sales world, making adjustments during and after a sales call will help the *sales professional* to improve. Successful *sales professionals* are often looked at as those who never do wrong. In reality, they have stumbled and fallen many times, only to pick themselves up, learn from their mistakes and move on to handle even greater challenges.

Senior Grandmaster Ed Parker had a ceremony at the end of every belt promotion that our Kenpo association still follows. At the very end of the test for your next rank, even at black belt, you are asked to kneel, placing your new belt and your old belt in front of you, forming an "L." Then, the head instructor explains what the "L" symbolizes. One of the things that the "L" stands for is "Lots to Learn". The holder of every new belt, including black belt, no matter what degree, always has more to learn.

Folded Belts Emphasizing Learning

A quote from Senior Grandmaster Ed Parker that reinforces the need to learn continually was:

"Anyone can be good with what little they know, but to

become better you must seek other truths that can be tailored to you."

When applied to the sales world, this quotation means that companies and sales forces have to have the same mindset. They must make it part of the company's culture, a passion, to learn continually and to make adjustments and refinements.

Companies and sales professionals <u>must</u> be passionate about learning. Continued Sales Education (CSE) has to be part of a company's culture and its own mindset. This is in contrast to what I have found with many of my former employers. When I suggested something that could be changed, improved or refined, I was told, "Don't rock the boat." This is the same mentality that many of the martial arts schools had before the first Ultimate Fighting Championship competitions. Once the UFC competitions started, those schools were easily defeated when their pupils were put up against a competitor who thrived in a realistic, constantly improving art.

Hundreds of years ago, martial arts masters would travel the world to study with other masters to add to their knowledge. The current mixed martial arts world does this every day, every week, over and over again. You can learn from many of the top experts in the world, with or without any travel, from articles, magazines, books, DVD's, seminars and the Internet.

One of my favorite sales resources, which was highly recommended by a presenter at a sales seminar I attended is the magazine "Selling Power," by Gerhard Gschwandtner, publisher. Mr. Gschwandtner exemplifies the MSA methodology of striving to learn and continually attempting to improve. His publication includes articles from sales professionals from numerous industries all over the United States and around the world. His website, SellingPower.com, has numerous newsletters specific to different sectors of sales. SellingPower.com offers webinars on different types of sales. How fortunate that you can spend time listening to presentations on building your sales from top sales executives, CXO's and sales consultants in America and around the world! (CXOs is now a common term used, because there are becoming so many variations of the term: CEO - chief executive officer, CFO - chief financial officer, COO - chief operations officer and CSO - chief sales officer.)

Many studies on sales back up the MSA methodology. Companies with formalized cultures of collaboration, i.e., exchanging of ideas, continued learning and improvement, usually rank higher in studies of companies' sales effectiveness. One study found that knowledge transfer (code word for collaboration, exchange of ideas or best practices) ultimately helps to increase a company's sales.

As mentioned previously, a key to continual learning is the threading of ideas. I was introduced to this term by Chris Kent, an expert in the martial arts specializing in Bruce Lee's Jeet Kune Do. He used the term a little differently, but when I called him and explained to him how I have used it to teach and learn the last few years, he agreed that my thinking was in line with his.

Many proven ideas can be used again and again in other areas. Once you learn an idea or a Truth, try to apply or thread it everywhere you can. For example, my term "increasing your odds" is a goal in both martial arts and sales. In martial arts, you are always trying to learn new moves and techniques that will "Increase your odds" of winning a competitive match or to survival in a self-defense situation. In the Closing Stage of sales, you are also trying to increase your odds of success. Once you've learned a key term such as always trying to increase your odds, you can thread it into many areas of the martial arts or sales.

Another example of threading a Universal Truth is revenue-generating activities. It should be the goal of every company to focus a majority of their sales force's time on revenue-generating activities that can or will have a high probability of producing added income. This is an idea that is and must be threaded throughout the **Strategic Selling Cycle.**

At my previous company, Collection Bureau, Inc. and Account Billing Service, the sales team had come up with an acronym. We were focusing on RGAs – revenue-generating activities, meaning we were trying to focus on activities that will bring in more business. This strategy implies that non-productive activities such as meetings that serve no true benefit, sales paperwork, sales reports, expense reports and other administrative activities preformed by sales professionals must be limited. Focusing on RGAs results in more time to be in front of prospects and customers, which in turn leads to more sales. If your sales force is partially commissioned, revenue- generating activities create more earnings for both the company and the sales professional. Now that is a win-win sales goal.

Companies need to develop a sales framework, a solid base and a company culture of striving continually to learn. Then they will be following the MSA methodology and will guarantee to "Improve Your Odds" in all your sales now and in the future. Many leaders in business have said that continual learning and innovation is the only sustainable competitive advantage in today's world of ultra competition. It is essential for survival!

3

Retention Strategy Stage

One of the most important keys to a Sales Professional's and company's success

Most forgotten stage in the sales cycle

I put retention first on the **Strategic Selling Cycle - SSC**, because it is one of the most important keys to a *sales professional's* and her company's success. It is also one of the most forgotten and neglected stages of sales. All companies should put it first on their sales cycle, as a reminder that existing profitable customers are one of the most important keys to their long term success.

Studies repeatedly show that it costs much more to attract a new customer than to retain one. Some studies show it costs as much as 40 times more to acquire a new customer vs. retaining an existing one. Wow! Again and again, companies seem to acknowledge that they are already aware of this fact. Other studies show that it is eight times easier to gain new business from an existing customer than business from a new customer. "Easier" is a code word for less time and money. Most companies acknowledge that they know this fact, too.

Senior Grandmaster Ed Parker told a story at his seminars which illustrates this point. He spoke of how a husband, who had a very beautiful wife, would go to a beach to enjoy the outdoors, sun and the ocean. The whole time, the husband would be looking around the beach, checking out other women. Many of these ladies were not even close to being as lovely as his wife, let alone as intelligent.

Senior Grandmaster Ed Parker's point was that many times we ignore great things that are right in front of our face. Many companies and *sales professionals* make the same mistake. They have some of the most lucrative customers right in front of their face but they fail to acknowledge these opportunities.

If a company has 500 existing customers and loses 15% of them a year, that is 75 customers. Now let's say your sales force brings in 75 new customers a year. Your growth is flat but your company has lost money. Since it costs less to sell to an existing customer and significantly more to sell to a new one, you have actually lost money while remaining at the same 500 customer base.

I was continually amazed by the mistake made repeatedly by most of my previous employers. To gain a new customer, they would bend over backwards and go the extra mile just to "get the business." The new prospective customer was a number one priority, but once that customer committed to the order or orders, the high-level service and focus was quickly forgotten.

> **BIG MISTAKE**
>
> **Forgetting your existing customers will help them forget you and your company.**

Recently, I ran across an advertisement in the classified section of our local newspaper. It was for a Retention Agent. It asked, "Do you know how to make the save?" They were looking for a motivated *sales professional* to help renegotiate contracts and agreements for customers that had been identified as at-risk. That ad really underscored the importance of customer retention. Since all the studies show that it is cheaper to keep an existing customer than to develop a new one, companies need to address the needs and concerns of their customers on a continuing and programmed basis.

The company that put the ad in the paper is on the right track, but the Retention Agent should be a step in their overall retention strategy. This is a great tactic for saving an at-risk customer, but there are many steps required before using a retention specialist.

Remember the 80% - 20% Rule in designing and implementing the retention strategy. Spend more time and resources for your top 20%.

The 80% - 20% Rule has existed for many years. It is a great idea that has been proven to be a *Universal Truth*. It implies that a majority of your revenues will come from a small percentage of your customers.

For many companies, losing one or two of the top 20% of their customers can have a devastating effect on their bottom line. Remember, it is much easier (code word for less money) to be proactive than reactive.

A Customer Relationship Management system (CRM) can help administer and automate many parts of the **Retention Strategy stage**.

Note: There is currently a lot of debate about CRM systems focusing more on the customer and Sales Force Automation (SFA) systems focusing more on improving sales results. The goal should be the same for both. I have used a CRM to improve both my relationship with my customers and help me improve my sales. We will leave the debate out of this book.

I will mention several times throughout this book that CRM systems are vital for all stages of the **Strategy Selling Cycle** in today's highly competitive business world.

You can apply the 80%-20% rule to the least profitable customers who are eating up a large share of a company's resources and profits. Some studies have found that the bottom 20% can eat up half of your profits! Companies have to focus on the top 20% while they make sure they do enough to retain the rest.

A good retention strategy helps with the **Support Stage** of the **Strategic Selling Cycle**. It lowers the cost of customer support by avoiding problems and/or the escalation of problems.

There are numerous low-cost ways to retain existing customers. Companies may offer special pricing incentives for existing and repeat customers; they can have reward programs with added discounts, prizes or perks; or they can periodically call the buyer at the customer's business to see if service is up to par. The personal touch does wonders for customer relations.

For the *sales professionals*, there are also numerous low-cost ways to retain customers. The total cost can vary by industry. For example, the pharmaceutical industry might spend several hundreds of dollars per customer, i.e., office lunches, numerous pens and office supplies with names of the particular drugs on them.

My goal in giving away any awards is to remind customers that my company and I appreciate their continued business. I am careful, though, not to cross the line of bribing or trying to buy their business. I think the integrity of a *sales professional* is a key to long-term success. Crossing the line, buying the business or bribing customers is a short-term strategy that frequently fails.

Consequently, I have always tried to show my appreciation with professionalism and integrity. I have done this by calling customers on a regular basis just to thank them for their business. For the most valued customers, I will try to have a face-to-face meeting to thank them for their continued loyalty. Keeping in touch with your customers is the most effective and least expensive retention tool.

Awareness

I have learned that utilizing and practicing "*awareness*" from my martial arts training also benefits me in becoming *aware* of issues with existing customers before they become a crisis.

Early on in my martial arts training, I was taught by Professor Hancock to be *aware* of my attitude and environment. Attitude meant paying attention to yourself both mentally and physically. For example, if you acted tired with your body slouching and an unfocused facial expression, it could appear to your opponent that you were close to quitting, which could become a self-fulfilling prophecy. If you paid attention to "yourself" and were "*aware*" of your attitude and actions, you would achieve more than you ever believed you could. The key was being *aware* of yourself, mentally and physically.

This is also true when you have interaction with your customers. If you are "*aware*" of your mental and physical actions and are positive and confident in what you say and in your physical appearance, your customer will have greater confidence in you and your company.

Next, being *aware* of your *environment* can help you avoid or head off problems before they become an emergency.

An example in the martial arts world would be a female walking to her car late at night in a parking lot by herself. Being *aware* of the dangers can help her "lower her risk" that night and in the future. One company I worked for made it a policy that a male employee would accompany each female employee to her car after dark. Taking such a precaution can be seen as being *aware* that there are risks and dangers but not being paranoid about them.

In the sales world, it is essential to be *aware* of your *environment*, prospects' and customers' actions, including their body language and what they say. Problems can be avoided just by being *aware*.

I have had a customer ask me "What are your rates again?" This is a red flag. Such a question can come up because a competitor has been in contact with the customer. Usually, I find out that my suspicions were correct. More than once, I have warned companies I worked for that I was *aware* that there might be a problem regarding a particular customer, only to be told that the particular customer would never use a competitor. Never say never. The customer soon went elsewhere with their business.

Continually working on awareness of yourself and your *environment* will help you significantly in both the *selling arts* and the martial arts worlds. Senior Grandmaster Ed Parker used to say, "There are those people who watch it happen, those who make it happen and those who ask, 'what happened?'" If you don't have and practice awareness, you and your company will be the ones asking, "What happened?"

By touching bases with a customer just to thank them for their business, you reinforce the relationship. The customer can be surprised in a good way by not trying to sell them something every time you want to talk with them. When you are just thanking them for their business, you are actually selling yourself and your company again in a creative way. You can also use this contact to find out important information, i.e., new key contacts and any unresolved issues.

Finding out that there has been a *change in guard* (new customer key contact) is <u>very</u> important. You now have an opportunity to introduce yourself, to set up a meeting to review the partnership between the two companies and to discuss past and future business. If this contact cannot be made in person, send a welcome and congratulations card. Then call to introduce yourself. Most importantly, use the opportunity to sell the new key contact on why their employer has chosen you and your company.

In the top twenty percent of your customers, if you find a *change in guard*, it is imperative that the *sales professional* has a meeting, face to face is best, with the new person. Face to face isn't always possible, so there should at least be a phone call. You want to help the new person to be successful and to start building a good relationship. Some new key contacts come from other companies in the same industry and have had previous relationships with competitors. *Change in guard* is an important concept and will be covered again in the **Prospecting Strategy stage**. Remember, in the *MSA - mixed selling arts methodology*, ideas such as *change in guard* are vitally important and can be *threaded* in other stages of the **Strategic Selling Cycle**.

When you make contact, if you uncover a customer need or unresolved issue, consider yourself lucky. This is an opportunity to help solve their or your company's problems. Your visit or call makes you and your company appear to be proactive, because the customer did not have to call you for help. Remember, many times customers will not call you with a complaint; they will just go to the competition.

Along with this technique of touching bases and saying thank you for their business, I often follow-up with a thank you card, coffee card to Starbucks® or drop off donuts or goodies. Nothing too expensive, just small tokens of appreciation. Sometimes I add a personal touch by sending birthday, new child and get well cards. This really helps build a special relationship with the customer. Keep in mind that many customers first think of the vendor they like when considering a need to make a purchase.

Usually, my top customers are very busy; and, a technique I use to get some quality, uninterrupted time with them is to offer to take them to lunch to discuss our partnership. I explain that I know they are very busy but that they will need to eat sooner or later. By allowing me to take them to lunch, we won't cut into their busy day. This is a great way to get the customer into a more relaxed environment. You can find out a good deal of useful information, while seeming to be talking about everything but business. This tactic is a good one, because your main focus is continually to build your relationship with the customer. These strategies and techniques can be *threaded* into other stages of the **Strategy Selling Cycle**, **Prospecting**, **Closing and Expanding stages**.

House Accounts

Many companies make the mistake of assuming that they have *house account* business forever secured. A *house account* is a customer that a company has determined to be in the bag. Many times they either don't have a *sales professional* assigned to the account or a busy executive of the company is supposed to be keeping in contact with them. Sure things do not exist in sales. In the early mixed martial arts competition, the commentators might say before the match, "This shouldn't be a long match." Today, the competition is so tough that you just can't take anything for granted. Valuable customer accounts require attention from knowledgeable and enthusiastic account managers, *sales professionals*.

It is in the best interests of the company and the sales force to focus on retention of all customers. When the sales force is not expected to be involved in *house accounts* and does not receive reasonable compensation for attention needed, loss of business is always a distinct possibility.

> **BIG MISTAKE**
> **House Accounts are like Fort Knox but without any guards!**

Everyone is in Sales

Every employee is selling your company each time they interact with a customer, regardless of the type of contact. There should be a sign posted in all companies displaying the two golden rules in sales:

> **Golden Rules...**
> **"Everyone in the company is in sales!"**
> **"It isn't what you say, but how you say it."**

A BIG MISTAKE made by most companies is allowing just any employee to interact with customers. There are some employees who are great at what they do but have NO business talking with customers. They just do not have the people skills needed to interact with customers.

I cannot count the number of times over the years that I have had to do *damage control* for something that a coworker said to a customer. "We just don't do that," rather than, "Is there another way we could accomplish the same thing?" "Your order is never going to make your deadline," rather than "Could we ship a partial order to get you by and the rest at a later date?" The examples are endless.

I am a big believer that every employee should go through sales training to help them understand that "Everyone is in sales" and "It isn't what you say but how you say it." Most *sales professionals* have been or should have been brought up learning these two principles. However, many employees have not been trained to recognize the importance of each and every customer.

Many managers give customer service lip service. Look on many company's walls and often you can find a plaque that states, "Customers are the number one concern." But then you overhear the manager, in front of other employees, say that a customer is too demanding.

29

Instead, he could have said that this is a challenging customer but she helps us pay our mortgage and car payments.

Every employee <u>has</u> to understand that they have a stake in the company's success and that customers' orders put bread on the table. *Sales professionals* having to put out fires lit by untrained coworkers mistakes keep *sales professionals* from focusing on *revenue-generating activities.*

> **BIG MISTAKE**
>
> **Allowing any untrained employee to interact with a customer or prospect is a mistake.**

Touch Points

A term that is common in the business world is *touch point*. It refers to what takes place every time the prospect or customer comes in contact with your firm. Companies need to make sure that their *touch points* are not on an electric fence. Companies need to scrutinize the various points where a customer can come into contact with them and their employees. These may include a website, customer service, storefront or accounting to name just a few. Companies must look at each point and make sure that the *touch point* is a very good experience for all prospects and customers.

Keeping in Touch

Sometimes a *sales professional* has an existing customer who is impossible to contact or who won't return calls. They always seem to be in a meeting. When a new order is received from that customer, it is a perfect time to try to make contact again. This illustrates the importance of a Customer Relationship Management (CRM) system. Many CRM systems can automate the notification of a new order to a *sales professional*. Now, the *sales professional* can call the customer to let them know that he/she noticed their order and wanted to thank them again for their business. At the same time, the *sales professional* can find out if there is anything else they need.

While working at Kinko's, later acquired by FedEx, I would deliver some orders myself, just to have an opportunity to meet and build my relationship with my customers. I was very specific as to which orders I delivered so as not to be seen by my coworkers as a backup delivery driver. *Sales professionals* need to make it clear that they need to focus their time on securing new business. Not doing so is a BIG MISTAKE.

I will cover this topic in detail in the **Fulfillment & Support Strategy stages**.

Frequently, the customer I thought might have been doing business with a competitor was really just too busy to meet with me. In such cases, the new order can put some of your concerns to rest. Additionally, new orders continually give you and your company another chance to earn customers' business by reinforcing your interest in them.

At many billing and collection agencies, the first of every month is the time when money is distributed that has been collected from the previous month. At these times, I review the list of clients who are receiving money from us. Then, I place phone calls to many of the customers and tell them to expect a nice check or direct deposit in the next few days and thank them again for their business. The customers are glad to hear from me and usually thank my company and me for all of our help.

I also make a list of strategic checks that fellow *sales professionals* and I will deliver in person. Another opportunity to keep in contact with the customer and they are very happy to see you. These contacts reinforce the customer's good decision in giving you their business.

While keeping in touch with your customers, you may discover critical information, such as a *change in guard*! If there has been a *change in guard*, you will make a memorable first impression by handing the new contact a nice sized check.

Delivering checks is also a great time to meet with customers who have stopped using your services, because they are trying to do the work in-house or they are trying out your competition. We will keep collecting money on past accounts for years, so this is a great way to thank them continually for their past business and to let them know we would love to help them out again. Happily, I have gotten many customers to return to us by using this technique. The competition makes promises that do not materialize and I make it easy and comfortable to request my company's services again. When they do make the decision to return to us, they are not embarrassed; because, I am continually touching base, either by e-mail, phone or in person.

Valued Resource

Another key to retention is for *sales professionals* and the company to be seen as valuable resources to the customer. There are many ways to accomplish this goal. The company can publish a newsletter with useful ideas for its customers and/or hold seminars on ways to help the customer to be more successful in their business.

I constantly read industry newsletters and magazines in order to share with customers new ideas and suggestions on how better to manage a company's accounts receivable. Also, I have met with hundreds of clients and have discovered best practices that are common between my customers.

Do not be just another vendor with some products and services to sell. The key is for you and your company to be viewed as a valuable resource by your clients. Constantly bringing ideas that will help the customer save money, make more money and make their job easier all help you to be a viewed as "valued resource".

KEY TAKEAWAY
Don't be just a friend to a client. Try to be a valued resource as well.

References and Referrals

References and referrals are earned through hard work. Any time I get an inquiry from a potential customer, I ask how they heard about our company. Sometimes, they mention the phone book or the Internet, but many times they have gotten our name from one of our existing clients. Even if they have told me they just got my name from the phone book, I will tell the prospect that I always ask because we get a lot of referrals and we consider that the ultimate compliment. If they were referred, I make a note of the referring person and company in my CRM system. I will then call that customer and thank them for the referral. I make sure to tell them those references and referrals are our company's ultimate compliment. Usually, the customers tell me that they were happy to do it, because we do such a great job. At this point, I will ask them if they mind my using their names for future references, so I can add them to my list of businesses on a reference sheet. Then, depending on several factors: potential of referral, size of current customer referring the lead, etc., I will send a follow up thank you card with a gift certificate as a small token of appreciation for the referral.

Companies need to encourage this type of behavior because referrals are a key to their success. I have had customers tell me that they refer me to everyone. I will ask for names of anyone they referred lately; and, if they didn't mind, I make a quick call and introduce myself. As mentioned earlier, businesses and people are busy and just might not get the time to call me. By taking the time to ask, I benefit by learning of new prospects. This is an example of where the stages overlap, and hard work in one stage benefits you in other stages.

> **KEY TAKEAWAY**
> **References and referrals are the ultimate compliment for any company!**

On numerous occasions, I have received communications letting me know the appreciation my customer has for my company's hard work or thanking me personally. The majority of the kudos the company and I have received have been short, informal and not always well written. Some have been thank you cards, which would not make good reference letters to give to a prospect.

When a customer repeatedly tells our company or me that we do a great job, it is a perfect opportunity to ask for a written letter of recommendation that can be used as a referral. Sometimes, companies tell me that we have helped them out a great deal and that if there is anything they can do for us to just ask. That is the moment that I will ask if they would consider writing our company a letter of recommendation. Although many experts have written that if you do a great job, a customer will write an unsolicited letter of recommendation, I see no reason to wait. When the time is right, I ask.

Asking for references might seem to be a simple thing, but creating a letter of recommendation takes time. To make it easy for the writer, offer to send them samples from other companies that have sent you letters. Coach them on what to include. This is key, because the stronger the letter of recommendation, the stronger prospecting tool it will become.

Companies and sales forces should always try to get referrals from industries that they are targeting for prospecting. Letters that are written by high-level people within a company and from companies that have name recognition will add to the strength of your references.

Follow up may be required to acquire these letters. When you have received one, immediately send a thank you card and a small token for their taking their valuable time to write you the letter. Usually, I will include a gift coffee card. The coffee cards might seem insignificant, but I get great feedback. The key is that it should be a small token of appreciation and industry appropriate.

Leverage

Brazilian Jiu-Jitsu is all about gaining and increasing your *leverage* while taking *leverage* away from your opponent. Most of the time, I have grappled much bigger opponents than me; and they often comment that I felt as though I weighed a ton. This is a compliment to me, because it lets me know that I was correctly using many aspects of *leverage* against them. The goal is to apply a move or technique successfully with less effort. Continually trying to find ways to increase your company's *leverage* is vital in the sales world too.

By following a retention strategy, you can *leverage* all the significant work you have done on building beneficial relationships and making your customers value you and your company's products and services. This *leverage* results in referrals and references, which are indespensible to gaining new customers in today's highly competitive business world. Your hard work in the **Retention stage** gives you and your company a huge head start in the **Prospecting stage**.

> **KEY TAKEAWAY**
> **Your and your company's success & profits are right in front of your face - your existing customers!**

Hopefully, you now understand the importance of making retention a top priority. The **Retention stage** needs to be listed first on any sales cycle for all the reasons stated. Remember Senior Grandmaster Ed Parker's story about the husband with the beautiful wife on the beach. Your and your company's success is right in front of your face in the form of your existing customers. Having a retention strategy is essential in today's business environment. Using some of the ideas presented here combined with your own, will *increase your odds* of keeping your valuable customers. Many companies make a BIG MISTAKE by finding excuses for not being focused on a retention strategy. Focusing on retention of existing customers may take time, but look again at the countless studies that found it takes a lot less time to keep a customer than to go out and acquire another one. By pursuing and maintaining a retention strategy, you will be following my personal motto in life, which is: "Working harder at working smarter."

4

Qualifying Strategy Stage

What does a good customer look like?

*Avoid prospects and customers
you and your company can't afford*

Learn the ABC's of rating your customers

The first step in the **Qualifying stage** is a quick evaluation of your target prospect. It is a high-level fly by view of where you look for types of potential customers who are a fit for your products and services <u>and</u> a fit for being a profitable customer. This step is similar to what many mixed martial artist fighters and promoters do before creating a match up. Research the competitor. Is it a good match up? Is it a fit?

You could go out as a fighter and take on any contest that comes your way. This may be OK at first; but, as you progress, you must be more selective if your goal is someday to be a champion.

In sales, if you want to go after just anyone as a prospect, get the phone book and start with A. This would be a BIG MISTAKE. Your goal in the **Qualifying stage** is to <u>narrow</u> your focus to potential customers who might be a good fit. Gradually, you have to narrow down the number of prospects. There are only so many hours in a day, and you have to *increase your odds*. The theme of increasing your odds will be *threaded* throughout the rest of the book.

> **KEY TAKEAWAY**
>
> **A goal of every company and Sales Professional is to try continually to "increase your odds" of success!**

In the early years of the UFC, Brazilian Jiu-Jitsu expert Pedro Carvalho, in one of his training DVD series, used the phrase "Big Mistake". Repeatedly, he would mention that trying a move or technique in a certain way at a certain time would be a "Big Mistake". This meant that there was a high probability that it would lead you into trouble. Since becoming aware of this phrase, I have used it as a tool to caution others about areas that have a high probability of failure or that will get you into trouble.

> **BIG MISTAKE**
>
> **Sales is a numbers game but don't play the lottery. Evaluate and eliminate!**

What does a good potential customer look like? A company and *sales professional* must have a basic profile in mind and they should be in agreement. Studies show that the business environment is becoming tougher to succeed in all the time, so it is more important than ever for companies to narrow down the prospect list. In many sales territories, there are hundreds if not thousands of prospects. Narrow them down and start to eliminate prospects that have a high probability of wasting the *sales professional*'s time. Ongoing studies have shown that over 60% of sales professionals are either pursing prospects that they can't close or <u>can't afford to close.</u>

It is necessary to define what a good prospective customer looks like. Just as in the **Retention stage**, you have to know who your profitable customers are in order for you to focus more of your resources on the most profitable ones. The first thing is to look at existing good customers. What do profitable customers have in common? Are they from similar industries? Are they of a similar size? Define the characteristics of your best customers and then build a picture of the ideal prospect.

Also, you must determine the characteristics of an unprofitable customer. This is an extremely important pursuit, since most companies want their *sales professional* to go after anyone who moves. Doing so is a BIG MISTAKE, as mentioned before. There are many prospects and some current customers that a company and the *sales professional* can't afford to have as a customer. Unfortunately, the unprofitable customer takes up too many resources in the **Fulfillment & Support stages**, and ends up costing the company and the *sales professional* money.

> **KEY TAKEAWAY**
> **True Profit = Revenue - Total Support Cost**

Many people would argue that this thought process is unfair, that it is supposed to be all about the customer. Well if it is, why don't you just give your products and services to all your customers for free? In reality, you have to make enough money to be able to stay in business, so you will be around to help all of your customers in the future.

In my current sales position, I do not solicit or prospect certain types of businesses. I have learned that although I have a high close rate with some types of businesses, they are unprofitable because of the level of support required. Revenue brought in is not the only determining factor. You must also consider, "How much will it cost the company and the sales professional to work with such a customer?"

According to Dictionary.com, one of the definitions of "qualify" is "To reach the later stages of a selection process or contest by competing successfully in earlier rounds." Once the *sales professionals* have a basic idea of what makes a good customer, they will be better able to focus their prospecting efforts in the right direction. Would your company reap a financial benefit from having this prospect if they were to become a customer? Not all prospects will be a fit for your company.

Rank your customers and prospects by potential. Just because a current customer is generating a fair profit, they might have the potential to move up from a level. On the other hand, if you have located a prospect in a dying industry who will require too much support and has very limited potential, should you really pursue them?

Categorize your income base by A - great customer, cash cow... profitable; B - customer, highly profitable; C - customer, profitable, D - worth having. Customers that rate below D do not always make the cut and should be gently discarded. When you are determining a customer's value in categories of A, B, C and D, the amount of resources and support required to maintain the customer has to be taken into consideration. One factor that I have used is a customer's name or brand recognition. I have retained many customers that are barely profitable, but their name gives your company and its products and services credibility.

Some customers are small to medium in size but have a nice profit to you and would be categorized as a B account, because they take so little support to maintain their business.

Taking time to categorize your customer base is critical in helping a *sales professional* be successful. To help qualify the true potential of a customer, you have to know the difference between *projects* and *programs*. A *project* is defined as a product or service that is usually a one time only sale or transaction. It does not have a high probability of repeating itself. A *program* is defined as a product or service that is recurring on a regular basis. Examples of *programs* are the servicing of a fleet of vehicles every 4,000 miles or printing a monthly newsletter for an organization. A goal for all *sales professionals* is to acquire *programs*. You have to work to get the initial sale of the *program* but then it results in multiple sales over time. *Projects* vs. *programs* is an important concept and will be *threaded* throughout other stages in the **Strategic Selling Cycle**.

Qualifying customers is a never-ending cycle. You should do this on a regular basis. In today's business environment, changes can and do happen at an ever increasing rate. A customer or prospect previously qualified and ranked as an *A* account could have shrunk to a *C* account. The reverse is also possible; a *C* customer may have grown into an *A* account.

KEY TAKEAWAY
Qualifying customers is a never-ending process.

5

Prospecting Strategy Stage

Environment is the first consideration

Cold calling works

Working harder at working smarter

Existing and dormant accounts

Just as the martial arts needs to change to meet the present realities of today's streets, so does the *selling arts* world need to change with current markets.

In the last five years alone, there have been huge changes in the business environment. It has become much more complex. Budgets have gotten tighter and there is more intense competition.

Studies have shown that when companies and their sales forces are surveyed about the selling *environment* for the next year, over 70 percent predict it will be a difficult to significantly difficult sales environment. Just as in the mixed martial arts world, competitors just keep getting tougher. The *basics* are the same in the MMA competitions with kicks, punches and grappling being used. In sales, the same *basics*, Retention, Qualify, Prospect, Close, Fulfillment, Support and Expand are still used. For success to be possible, the *basics* in both areas will need to be augmented by more sophisticated techniques and strategies.

Environment

Senior Grandmaster Ed Parker said that the *environment* is the number one consideration in a self-defense situation. He stated that the *environment* is what is <u>in you</u>, <u>on you</u>, and <u>around you</u>. Examples: "In You" might be that you are sick, which would affect your ability to defend yourself. "On You" could be a heavy belt, which could be used to help defend yourself. "Around You" might imply that it is icy where you are and high kicking would be risky. Examples of businesses having an understanding of their *environment* in the sales world: "In You" could be alcohol at an event with customers. This might affect the way you interact professionally with the customer. "On You" could be the way you are dressed, professional vs. tacky. "Around You" could be your company's negative *environment*, which would affect the way you sell. The examples are endless, but the idea is invaluable, both in martial arts and in business.

The *environment* concept is an essential tool and can be *threaded* throughout the **Strategic Selling Cycle**.

The business environment is changing at a rapid pace and has to be the first consideration before a company's sales force heads in any direction.

Prospecting has become more difficult because of today's business environment. Prospects are being bombarded with solicitations by mail, phone, email, computer pop ups, walk-ins, radio ads and TV ads.

In MMA competition, you can't dictate all phases of your *environment*: size of ring, type of matting, etc. It is the same in the business world. Most of the "around you" factors outside of your company are out of your control. Having an understanding of the *environment* around you will help your company and its sales forces develop "best practices" strategies, so they can prospect more effectively. Care should be taken not to accept strategies, ideas or techniques until they have been proven to work for your company. Consider them and try them, but don't make them the basis of your game plan until you are confident that they work.

KEY TAKEAWAY

"If the rate of change on the outside of the firm exceeds the rate of change on the inside, the end is near."

Jack Welch, Former General Electric chairman and CEO

Many leading sales experts, authors and consultants feel that prospecting through cold calling is, to quote several, "A total waste of time". I disagree. My experience with cold calling and strategic cold calling in seven different industries is that strategic cold calling works! A weekly business column that runs in the local newspaper agrees. Rhonda Abrams states in her article on cold calling, "Here is the dirty little secret: Cold calls works." (Rhonda Abrams, president of The Planning Shop, publisher of books, www.planningshop.com)

In the early years of the MMA competitions, kicking was not very successful. Many of the "experts" said that under realistic conditions kicks just did not work, especially head kicks. Now, years later, they are a necessary part of a total fighter's package. Frequently, victories are the result of head kicks. The well-rounded fighters know all the ranges and the *set up* before attempting kicks.

Some keys to prospecting are attitude, passion and planning. You have to keep a good attitude even with rejection. You must be passionate about your products or services and you need to have a plan of attack. Lack of planning is part of the reason sales forces have such poor results in prospecting. As mentioned earlier, one of the goals of sales is to continually strive to *increase your odds*. Even with proper planning, prospecting takes perseverance and a great attitude. You are trying to *increase your odds*, not guarantee your odds. As one of my sales managers used to say, "You are going to hit a few in the weeds". Yes, even golf great Tiger Woods hits a few in the weeds. However, my goal is to hit fewer in the weeds than my competitor.

A great attitude combined with passion is cited by many in the sales world as keys to any sales professional's success. I agree! However, I have heard more than one mixed martial arts trainer say, "A fighter with passion and a great attitude alone is looking for a beating." You need skills along with attitude and passion to become a great competitor in the MMA or the MSA - *mixed selling arts* world.

It is best to hire persons with a great attitude and to teach them the needed skills, since having a great attitude and positive outlook are difficult to teach. One person who best summed up the importance of a great attitude was Lou Holtz, college football coach and motivational speaker.

> ### KEY TAKEAWAY
> **"Ability is what you're capable of doing, Motivation determines what you do. Attitude determines how well you do it."**
>
> **Lou Holtz, football coach and motivational speaker**

The **Prospecting stage** will cross over into other stages of the **Strategy Selling Cycle**, but let's focus on strategies and techniques to get a meeting with the prospect. I have found that my close rate goes up significantly with a face-to-face meeting vs. phone, mail, and all other contacts.

Studies have shown that many *sales professionals* are working harder and not smarter, more calls and more hours worked to get an appointment or close a deal.

Experience has demonstrated the need for companies, sales organizations and all employees to strive to be "Working harder at working smarter". Certainly, you have to work hard; but there comes a point when you achieve diminishing returns. That is where working smart comes into play. Nowhere is this more important than in prospecting.

When I worked for Moore Business Forms, I had a meeting with my boss and his superior. At lunch, the new regional manager asked me if one of the other *sales professionals* in our district put in 60 hours a week, would I be willing to work 65 to beat them. I calmly said no. He looked shocked. I told him I already worked very hard but was "Working harder at working smarter." He wasn't very happy. He was what I would call old school, Sales 1.0, or the wrong school. Sales success has taught me that "Working harder at working smarter", Sales 2.0, is the real key to sustainable long-term sales growth.

Another wonderful saying about the need for working smarter is this:

One of the first steps to prospecting, "What does a good customer look like?" should be done early on in the **Qualifying Strategic stage**.

> ### KEY TAKEAWAY
> **"Rowing harder doesn't help if the boat is headed in the wrong direction."**
>
> **Kenichi Ohmae, management consultant**

Next is "where is the best place to find them?" Then comes "how can I communicate with them?" and finally, "how can I meet with them face to face?" Those are the *basics*. Now, let's sophisticate the *basics* to *increase your odds* of success!

Always Be Prepared!

Know and practice what you are going to say before you talk to any prospect. Just as in any MMA competition, you will have practiced your moves and your responses to opposing moves numerous times before you meet your opponent. In the mixed martial arts you have to identify your competitors' strengths in order to formulate a game plan before the fight.

I am amazed that when I ask some of the MMA competitors about their next fight, they have little or no knowledge of their next opponent. In the top levels of competition in the MMA world, top competitors study and strategize game plans before every fight. The MMA competitor also has to have proper gear: mouthpiece, gloves, gloves taped, groin protector and shorts when they step in the ring. These are the basics for any competitor.

The same needs exist in the sales world. Knowing your competitors' strengths and weaknesses beforehand substantially helps *increase your odds*. You must prepare and practice <u>what</u> you are going to say and <u>how</u> you are going to say it before you speak to your prospect. Nothing can reduce your odds more than sounding unprofessional the first time you talk to your prospect. Bad first impressions will significantly reduce your chances of getting an appointment or any business at a future date. When you meet a prospect, you have to be dressed appropriately and be prepared with a pen and paper, your calendar/schedule and business cards. These are just the simple prerequisites.

I have been apprehensive about using pre-set or pre-arranged moves in martial arts or in sales. Many times in both, the moves are just too complicated and unrealistic for the real world. However, I have learned that pre-set moves based on *Truths* can succeed. These are moves that work most of the time, have been tested under pressure and under realistic conditions, not just in martial arts schools or sales training classrooms.

I have been prospecting for over 20 years and I still rehearse, at least mentally, what I am going to say.

Here is a saying I enjoy, "Ninety percent of success is just showing up." Accordingly, showing up prepared will substantially increase your chances of success.

Being prepared includes keeping all the necessities with you, e.g., business cards, pen, calendar, PDA, samples, sales literature, letters of recommendation and anything else you might need while you are out of the office. If you make enough sales calls, you will find that always being prepared helps secure extra sales with little effort.

Existing Accounts

It is smart to prospect first with existing accounts. Studies show that it is significantly easier to sell to an existing customer. We will cover prospecting existing accounts in detail in the **Expanding Strategy stage**. Next should be dormant accounts. Your chances of success will be higher, because you usually have some prior information about the customer.

Dormant Accounts

Revisiting dormant accounts can be a very profitable venture for both a company and their *sales professionals*. It should be part of any company's **Prospecting Strategy**.

Dormant accounts are defined as those customers who have not done business with your company for some amount of time. The time will be determined by the business or industry. In my current industry, billing and collections, most customers will typically give us accounts monthly or quarterly. If a customer had a history of turning over new accounts to our company every month and it has been six months to a year, they would be considered a dormant account.

Dormant account reviews should be part of any company's "Retention Strategy", but several of the companies I have worked for did not have dormant account reviews as part of any strategy. In my current position, it is easy for me to have a reason to go see a dormant account. I might have a check for them from their old accounts and I can deliver the check in person or call to see if they received our check. This helps to get my foot back in the door. This was one of my first focuses when I started working my previous billing and collection employer. As a result, I was very successful at reactivating dormant accounts. Some required me to resell our services, but the odds were in my favor compared to selling a completely new prospect.

Periodically, Kinko's, now FedEx Office, would send out dormant account lists, but they could have done a better job by fully training the sales force on the best ways to utilize the information.

Frequently, they would have the inside *sales professional* send letters or call the customers to gain their business back. The cost of the inside *sales professional's* time would have been better spent working with the outside *sales professionals* and others in the company with insight into the true potential of a customer.

Kinko's was on the right track by running reports of customers' spending habits. It was amazing to see how much or how little a customer spent. These reports were an invaluable tool for sales, not only on dormant customers but also on existing ones. Much of this monitoring could and should be automated to flag the company if a customer has not ordered in a particular time period. Many CRMs (Customer Relationship Management systems) can accomplish this type of automation.

Once dormant accounts are qualified, they need to be sorted into *A, B, C* and *D* accounts. Many of the dormant accounts on the list wouldn't make the cut of being categorized as a *D* account, because of their spending history and were qualified as having no growth potential. A determination must be made as to what size dormant accounts are worth spending resources to regain their business. To truly qualify some accounts, ground troops are needed, i.e., *sales professionals* to investigate. On accounts with less potential, maybe sending them a coupon for a next purchase might be in order. Automated bulk mailing or an email blast would be less expensive than having the *sales professionals* waste their limited and valuable time hand mailing a letter and/or making a phone call. The time to pass dormant accounts on to your sales force is after they have been qualified.

When I was a Corporate Account Manager at Kinko's, I was recognized for having the largest percentage of growth in my territory out of the entire United States sales force. This was largely accomplished by focusing a big part of my **Prospecting Strategy** on dormant accounts that might have been overlooked by the company.

I have evaluated dormant accounts and decided that it would be worth a phone call or visit to investigate if the customer's true potential had been overlooked. I have used my *"Just want to give you a quick update"* technique to get an appointment while prospecting. Then, I told the customer that I wanted to give them some valuable information that would be beneficial in their business. Additionally, I offered them some coupons for future purchases. All *sales professionals* have to be "P.I.'s" - private investigators. A little investigation on the account is needed, and someone in your company should be able to give you insights to better understand the customer. Being a private investigator is a critical role for any *sales professional* who wants to be at the top of his/her game.

KEY TAKEAWAY
All great Sales Professionals have to be their own "P.I.", Nancy Drew or Sherlock Holmes.

I used the technique of focusing on dormant accounts successfully again when I worked for ITG -Intermountain Technology Group. I started just before 9/11. After that, the "heyday" of ITG and all IT companies would be forever changed. Sales became very difficult to make. Other veteran *sales professionals* were already handling many of the good accounts and many companies had no budgets to buy anything new.

I would call dormant accounts and use my "*Just want to give you a quick update*" technique; but, before I called, I would check the CRM system for past history. Then, I would ask around ITG to see if anyone knew anything about the customer. I would try to get some *intelligence* about the customer company, key contact and any type of information that could help when making the call. Being able to drop a name often helped turn a cold call into a *warm call*, which is another technique I used in combination with "*Just want to give you a quick update.*" (Remember, all moves are *connected.*) These tactics are vital because of the amount of unrequested solicitation many prospects receive on a daily basis. You do not want to just be another blind solicitation.

"*Just want to give you a quick update*" and "Turn a cold call into a *warm call*" techniques are *threaded* throughout other stages of the **Strategic Selling Cycle** and are techniques that I call *high percentage moves*.

The "*Just want to give you a quick update*" is a great technique for a less threatening *approach*. When making your initial contact by referring to someone they know who had past dealings, hopefully you have a previous relationship bond. Then, by mentioning what you have done and how you have helped other recognizable companies gains you a little creditability.

While working for several companies, I found out that the true potential of some customers was overlooked. Many times, the customer did not have a need at an earlier time or there was a poor job done qualifying the true potential of the customer.

Where are you going to find more prospects once you have existing and dormant accounts handled? There are numerous strategies and techniques that can be used, depending on your industry, type of business and geographic location. The following are some *Truths* and *Universal Truths* I have discovered from my diverse experience in B2B Professional Sales.

Networking

Many sales experts will advise, "Never stop networking." Utilize family, friends, business associates, go to any and all networking events and trade shows you can. I disagree with many of those experts a majority of the time.

Who is your *target audience*? If I mention to friends and or associates that I am in sales for a particular company, they talk to me about a small, personal, *project* they are thinking about. I discuss it with them and many times they want me to help them with the *project*. Most think they are doing me a favor by giving me some business. Remember the difference between a *project* and a *program*. I am always polite, but I tell them there is an expert in our company who handles this type of work. Then, I pass them on to an inside *sales professional*, who can help them over the phone or by email. Additionally, I give them coupons for products and services for any future business.

The hope is that you will pick up a lot of new business by telling everyone what you do, or the person you talk to will introduce someone who will be a great lead. Remember the difference between business-to-business (B2B) and business-to-consumer (B2C). In B2B sales, it takes a prospect who can buy substantial amounts of business to be placed on to my account list. None of my personal friends are going to place a $50,000 order as many of my customers do on a continual basis. Most, if not all, B2C would never make it on the list.

I have found that my *target audience* is a very select group.

As I stressed in the **Qualifying Strategy stage**, you do not want everybody as a customer. There are more prospects and customers that you "Can't Afford to Close" than ones that you truly can and want to secure as a new customer.

A classic mistake at many networking events is not recognizing the differences between B2B vs. B2C sales. Do not forget to do the numbers. B2B *sales professionals* have large monthly goals and need businesses that spend thousands of dollars a year. Most individuals are not going to purchase the volume needed to make your numbers. Many of the networking events do have *sales professionals* that search out both B2B and B2C sales. Some examples are: Mortgage and insurance brokers, financial advisors, insurance agents, chiropractors, etc. *Sales professionals* who sell B2C products and services benefit a lot more from most networking events if people show up. That is their *target audience*.

If you attend an event, or bump into a person who might help you locate a prospect who fits your profile of an A, B, C, or D customer, then by all means network. Over the years, I have found that my *target audience* doesn't show up at most networking events. But a lot of sales people do and "we" *sales professionals* are not usually good B2B prospects.

Jill Konrath is founder, CSO, of SellingToBigCompanies.com and she has written on the subject. She tends to agree with my past experiences and said it best, "Stop networking and start calling".

Networking by *sales professionals* should be focused on networking with customers. Talk to them about people and businesses they know who can benefit from your products and services. If you have a good relationship with the customer, ask if they can recommend a person who will be best to contact? May you use your customer's name as a reference?

Keep your eyes and ears open at social events and by all means, prospect. Typically, top executives will be interacting with each other at events that your standard *sales professional* wouldn't even be attending. This is where my saying is never truer, "Everyone is in sales". A high level person of your company can help get you a warm lead. However, the executive level VIPs of your company need to know how to facilitate a good lead. Some of the most successful companies have top executives who understand that they are also in sales. Your company's executives do not have to sell their companies' products and services to the another executive, but they should sell the importance of having their decision makers for the particular product and service talk to a *sales professional* from your company. This is where "top down" selling makes sense.

> **BIG MISTAKE**
>
> **Companies and sales forces not understanding the difference between B2B and B2C.**

Trade Shows

Many companies spend valuable dollars to have a booth at a trade show; but in the industries I am familiar with, I have not seen much benefit from using such a booth. If you are looking for exposure in your industry, a trade show booth might be a useful option. Just make sure your *target audience* is going to come to that type of trade show.

There are benefits to simply attending trade shows. As an individual, I have gone to numerous trade shows looking for leads and I have had some success using this technique. Going to a trade show helps you network by putting you in a buyer perspective. You are able to gain more information, because the company representatives are not always experienced *gatekeepers* and tell more than ask. It also helps you to see what the competition is doing by going to their booths to investigate. I find that industry-specific trade shows are beneficial when looking for prospects. Then, the people coming to the trade show are from a particular industry and looking for information about products and services for that industry. It narrows the prospect pool to people with identifiable interest.

At my present employer, we have been successful with a strategic *approach* to industry-specific conferences where a trade show is going to be part of the conference. We plan strategic steps to ensure that trade shows yield us value for the expenses we incur by going. Both the monetary cost and the cost of your time all have to be taken into consideration. What exactly are we looking to accomplish? Is it to gain new prospects? Build relationships with existing customers? Gain more exposure for our company? How are we going to accomplish our goals?

Many people come by your booth, not to look at your company's products and services, but to get goodies like candy, pens, letter openers and drawings for prizes. Therefore, one of our first goals is to determine how to get more real prospects and existing customers to stop by our booth.

We acquire a list of attendees and mail a postcard to all of those on the list stating, "We look forward to seeing you at the conference." Of course, our company's name is all over the postcard; and more importantly, we let them know that they have two chances now to win our giveaways. The first chance to win is to drop off a business card into our entry box at our company location. Then, they can get a second chance by bringing our postcard and dropping it off at our booth. Also, having goodies, candy and little giveaways is helpful in getting people to drop by your booth, which gives you a chance to approach them.

One of my sales team members takes the list of all the planned attendees and color-codes them by existing customer, existing prospect or new prospect. That way, we are prepared when we arrive at the trade show. As a final step, once the trade show or conference is over, we *follow up* on leads and *next steps* to ensure a return on investment of the company's money and our time invested.

Hosting Events

I have found that hosting an event brings the prospects to you. At ITG - Intermountain Technology Group, the sales manager's thinking was right on and ahead of his time. He preferred to create events to bring the prospects to us. We would host seminars on specific companies' solutions, Microsoft, Symantec IT security and VERITAS Storage to name a few. I was in charge of one of the Microsoft events and it ended up with standing room only. I accomplished this in the standard way ITG had always promoted these gatherings and added my own technique to enhance the event's success. Previously, the marketing department did an email blast out of their CRM system (Customer Relationship Management) to all the contacts in their CRM system database. I will say again and again that fully utilizing a CRM system is a must for the success of any company in today's intensely competitive environment.

After the email blast, I made a list of key accounts and key prospective accounts and made sure that the email information promoting the event was emailed to the correct contacts. In our existing CRM system database, I frequently found that information such as email address or contact name had not been updated. The goal was not only to get a large group of people to the event but also to get the right people. I took care to make sure that all of the other *sales professionals'* current prospects received the email invitations as well.

Next, in order to make sure the customers were sold on the importance of coming to the event, I called up any key customers who the other *sales professionals* had not called. I tried to create excitement about the happening, and I utilized a variation of my "*Just want to give you a quick update*" technique. "You might not need this product right now but the information is vital to future planning."

Lastly, on the day before the event, I called and reminded all the key contacts who had committed to attend the event. I said, "Once again, I need to stress the importance of attending the event." Later,

I was told by my sales manager that the company usually had a 50% drop off from the RSVPs. He also said that by contacting some of the RSVPs to assure that they came to the event, we could expect 80% of committed RSVPs to attend.

Online seminars and webinars do a good job of providing memory cues. They will email your reminders the day before and the day of the event. This is all programmed to happen automatically. However, since ITG - Intermountain Technology Group seminars were local events, I think a combination of email and phone calls served our company the best. In the end, I had over 90% attendance from the RSVPs. All of the *sales professionals* from our company had to stand because the seats were full; and we even had to squeeze in a few extra seats. Following my steps in preparing for other events proved to be equally successful.

A special event is a great way to get prospects and customers outside of their *environment* and into one that is a bit more relaxed. They get to have a little time off with refreshments, and they gain information useful for their own position and their company's.

There are many details involved in hosting an event like this that will give you the biggest bang for your buck. For example, make sure you greet the customers and have them sign in. Having their name, title, company's name, phone number and email address helps you confirm the information that is in your CRM system database. This makes it easier for the attendees than to fill out some long questionnaire. For any new prospect who might show up, you need to make getting their information as painless a possible. Ask for their business card.

Always have a feedback questionnaire at the end of the event. Try to keep it positive but ask for suggestions to help your company bring in experts and to cover beneficial topics. Provide a line on the questionnaire to see if they would like more information, even though most people know this is a solicitation technique.

The last but critical step is to have the sales professionals follow up with the attendees while there is still excitement. I have used this strategy and technique at my past employer. I had Mark Clark, attorney at law for over thirty years and twenty years experience in the collection industry, give seminars for associations on collections and the law. It was very successful, and I have found this strategy to be a Truth. In addition, I have gained several valuable customers from these events and I have increased the exposure of our company.

A cautionary note: Live and online seminars are great prospecting tools, but they have to provide valuable and beneficial information. Unfortunately, many such events seem to be sales pitches in disguise that have little substance.

Informal Events

You can also host an informal event; take a prospect to a sporting event, concert, dinner or other social event. This is a great way to build a relationship outside of the normal, hectic business environment. These occasions are typically after normal business hours. A term I have used for years is *schmoozing* the prospect. It is a slang term, for thanking and rewarding customers for their existing or future business. As I mentioned in the **Retention Strategy stage**, there is a fine line between courting a prospect or customer and bribing one. You have to think strategically: What are you and your company trying to accomplish? Are you trying to build a relationship? Do you want to improve a relationship? You do not want to talk much about business at such a time. Of course, it's fine if the customer brings up business; but for the most part, the main focus of these outings is to build a relationship of trust with the customer. Remember, at any event like this, it is *environment* first, what is in you? In other words, limit the alcohol to a maximum of one or two drinks.

Many times, the customer never brings up business; but the orders start to come in at a later date. A number of techniques and strategies overlap and can be applied in several areas of the **SSC**. Also, these informal events are highly recommended for the **Retention Strategy stage**.

Webinars

Online seminars are becoming more popular, and they are commonly called webinars. These are very similar to the events I have been involved with in the past, except they are done over the Internet. I have attended numerous webinars through my involvement with *Selling Power* magazine.

Webinars are very useful tools to enable companies to hold cost-effective seminars. Webinars are also very valuable from a potential customer's point of view. Companies can give online seminars on particular subjects. I have attended webinars on sales hosted by top executives of sales for very large and/or progressive companies. They usually last only one hour at lunch time, so I find them easy to fit into my schedule. I can often pick up a new idea or two from a webinar.

Many times, the sponsor will be a software company that is promoting its software for webinars or online conferencing.

All this is done on the Internet from your PC and can be viewed from a location anywhere in the world. I predict the use of webinars will become a standard practice for delivering all types of information. Online seminars will be and are a way to provide *Customer Continued Education (CCE)* strategy, which will be covered in detail in a later section.

In some webinars, you can type in questions to a moderator during the presentation, and they are usually answered during the webinars. These online seminars are becoming a cost effective way to prospect to any type of potential customer, especially over a large geographical area or even around the world. The goal is the same as an in-person seminar: to inform and then to persuade the listening audience members to take some type of action.

Snail Mail Prospecting Letters

Sending out prospecting letters has been done by several of my previous employers, all with similar results. Very little to none. This is a method of cold calling through the mail. I have been involved in mailing letters, manually and partially automated; and all have had poor results. Also, sending letters, brochures and catalogs is getting more expensive because of the time and cost of mailing hard copies.

I am always amazed that *sales professionals* will try to solicit my business by sending me very expensive brochures and catalogs that I just throw in the trash. Worse yet, many send me these items and never *follow up*! This is a very BIG MISTAKE, because, *follow up* is one of the most important <u>keys</u> to sales success. Any *sales professional* who wants to be at the top of his or her game will have to do outstanding *follow up*. I will cover the importance of *follow up* and the concept will be *threaded* through several stages of the **SSC**.

I read an article from a former sales manager who told his sales team, when trying to make a point, that every sales brochure packet sent out would cost them five dollars out of their own pockets. He was trying to help his sales team understand the need to use the company's money wisely.

> **BIG MISTAKE**
> **Poor follow up is the quickest way to start playing the lottery.**

When I was with Kinko's, we did a letter campaign and then I made follow up calls. All of the prospects said they did not receive my letters. Consequently, I realized that I would have been better off not to have spent the time to send the letters but to have spent more time finding the right person to call. I had similar experiences at Simplex.

When I worked at ITG, we had a former top *sales professional* for NEC come in and talk about his technique of sending letters. This was done ten to twenty years before he was talking to us. He sent the letters to CXO's and told us that he received great results and recommended that our whole sales force do the same. There were seven *sales professionals* listening. I told my sales manager that I would do as recommended but felt from past experience that we would get little to no results.

Each one of the *sales professionals* was supposed to send out a minimum number of ten letters to CXO's at our top prospecting accounts. I sent the letters and followed up but was ignored.

Not one of our *sales professionals* received an appointment by sending out the letter campaign.

This technique might have worked twenty years ago, combined with the name recognition of NEC at that time; but it was not effective and would be considered a *"low percentage move"* in today's business environment.

Some experts will say letter campaigns are effective because you can track your results. I agree with being able to track success and that is why mailing unsolicited letters just has not been one of the *high percentage moves* that I have used in my 20 years of sales. For me, this technique has turned into a *specialized move* and works only in very special, targeted situations.

Incoming Phone or Email Inquiries

Companies should have a system in place for incoming calls, emails, and leads to be qualified before passing them along to outside *sales professionals*. Most companies do not do a good job of training and putting a system in place to screen incoming inquiries. Training is necessary for all personnel taking incoming inquiries to evaluate the prospect and to handle them efficiently. If inside employees cannot truly evaluate, at least pass them on to a qualified inside *sales professional* to assist, further investigate and qualify. Then, and only then, pass inquiries to outside *sales professionals.*

As mentioned earlier, fully qualifying a prospect over the phone can be difficult. In those cases, it might be necessary for an outside *sales professional* to visit the company. At Kinko's, inquiry calls were passed to me. If I couldn't determine the prospect's potential on the phone and it sounded as though there might be a reasonable opportunity, I would schedule a meeting and do a site visit.

Just as in the military, you often need the ground troops to get a clearer picture of the battle situation. It is the same in sales and I would attempt to train fellow employees on the characteristics of a good prospect. Such training would limit some of the B2C incoming calls from being forwarded to me.

During my time at Kinko's, I would go to the prospect's place of business to do further qualifying. If there was not a fit for a dedicated outside *sales professional,* I would tell the prospect I was a liaison for Kinko's, give them a quick update, some coupons, and thank them for their inquiry. For any of their future business needs, I would give them an inside *sales professional's* business card. These prospects or customers were very happy with our follow up; and usually a relationship would start up for future business. The upcoming business would be supported in a cost-effective manner. A dedicated *sales professional* is very expensive for a company and must have customers that bring in enough profit to justify the costs.

Internet Listings and Phone Books

I have received phone call inquiries where the callers have gotten our company name from an online phone directory or a phone book. At such a time, it is important to ask where the prospect heard about us. Inquiring every time is important to see where your leads are coming from. In my experience in B2B sales, I have not spoken to many A or B type prospects who have picked our company's name from the phone listing. Typically, a good prospect will ask a business associate for help in locating names of vendors who might be able to help them. These are called referrals, not blind inquiries. It is certainly an option to have an advertisement in the major phone listings of your area, but don't expect it to be a major source of good quality B2B lead generation.

Directory listings are most beneficial to B2C companies, such as plumbers, attorneys, chiropractors, etc.

Company Website

Any commercial website needs to be well thought out. Remember the importance of first impressions? If your company website is not set up and maintained properly, it could be the prospective customer's first and last impression.

This is an area where I look for help from an expert. I have worked for several companies that have had websites; but, from a sales perspective, I have seen little personal benefit.

On the other hand, I once attended a webinar and a *sales professional* followed up with me. When I asked him about his firm's lead-generation process, he said that he received leads from both the company website and webinars. The leads were pre-qualified by the size of the company and the level of the prospect's position in the company. His company had a department whose sole responsibility was to analyze, qualify and pass on leads. This company has done what many others need to duplicate.

During the last couple of years many *Truths* and best practices have been uncovered regarding website construction and on-going maintenance. A number of experts agree that your company's website should reflect your company image, be easy to use and navigate to locate information and have a simplified system for making a purchase from your company.

I have found there are two main types of company websites or a combination of the two. First is the website which provides general information about your company. This may be of little importance to the prospective customer. It should contain general information concerning your products and services, along with contact information for making a purchase or gaining future information.

The second type is one that is an online storefront. The Dell Computer website is a good example of this type. Dell.com, like many online stores, provides for an online chat to help with customers' questions. This type of website allows customers to get information easily online and to make their purchases directly on the Internet.

Marketing

Historically, marketing departments have used a shotgun approach to get their company's messages to the largest number of people possible. However, my experience is that most companies still confuse B2B and B2C customers. A shotgun effect on B2B prospects is not the best use of advertising money. Much of the marketing material that I have been given to use in my previous sales positions was too general to be useful. The fancy brochures and commercials look nice, but many times I couldn't figure out what message the marketing department was trying to get across.

If marketing departments truly want to provide tools to help a B2B sales force, they need to narrow their focus and message to what matters most to the *target audience*. They should focus on the sales force's top 20 percent of prospects and customers, rather than trying to send out a broad message that does not resonate with anyone. More marketing departments need to ask "What does the prospective customer want our company to help them accomplish?" Then, they need to work backwards from that point.

Marketing and sales departments that work together accomplish the best results. Sales forces work daily with prospects and customers and should know the key customer concerns. Also, how does marketing track its success? The sales department has a quota, but does marketing track its success? From my experience, these departments have not done very well unless they have worked together. My thinking must be accurate, because Bill McDermott, CEO and President of SAP America has said, "In the most successful companies, marketing and sales work as one." Mr. Dermott should know. Since joining SAP, the company has seen tremendous growth worldwide.

In the past, the sales manager or I have made up the marketing tools I have been able to effectively utilize. Why do you think that is? It is mainly because we are at the ground level, listening to customers' needs and problems on a daily basis.

Marketing, at least B2B marketing, has to work closer with the sales force. Have the marketing personnel ever been on a sales call with a *sales professional?* If not, then it will be tough to truly know the problems customers need help overcoming. Companies have to remember that the marketing department's involvement is an important step of the **Prospecting Strategy stage**.

Lead Generation

Leads come in many shapes and sizes. You can pick up some from trade shows, hosted events, networking, webinars, company websites, email and letter campaigns, marketing, existing customers and phone listing advertisements.

Companies have to have a plan to generate, handle and manage their leads. I have worked for large, international companies that have passed leads on to fellow *sales professionals* and me that have been a total waste of valuable selling time. The leads have been old, contact information limited and source limited. Where did the lead come from? When I did finally find the right contact, they would struggle to remember that they put a business card in for a free prize months previously. With a few qualifying questions, I would "Evaluate and Eliminate" them as a prospect.

Good leads can come from within. Some of my best leads were from our company's non-sales service people who had interacted with the customers in the field. Utilizing fellow coworkers is one of my personal keys to success in sales.

There are internal and external customers. *Internal customers* are called fellow coworkers. When I worked at ITG, our technicians and engineers were very hard workers. They toiled many long hours, many times on overtime, to complete projects before a deadline. I always would go out of my way to treat these people with respect, and I always thanked them for all their hard work. Many times, they would be working on a project and I would ask them what they were doing for lunch. They might tell me they had to work through their lunch hour, so I would pick them up a sandwich from one of the national chains I frequented. I'd tell them this was just a small token of my appreciation for all the hard work they had done for me. Now, when they had a lead from a customer, who do you think they usually gave it to? You guessed it, the person who showed them a little gratitude and respect. As I saw it, they were my customers, too.

You do have to coach your fellow coworkers on what a good lead is. Again, I am a specialist in B2B sales. Many times fellow coworkers would think that any lead was a good lead, and I would have to constantly educate them on what a good lead looked like. B2C almost always was NOT what I consider to be a good lead.

KEY TAKEAWAY

Treat both internal and external customers well. Internal customers are known as "fellow coworkers".

There have been several studies done over the last few years which have concluded that *sales professionals* themselves generate almost half of all leads. The rest are split up by other sources.

Most companies that I have worked for did a poor job of lead generation and I have been my own chief lead generator. From taking a poll on www.SellingPower.com of *sales professionals'* best sources for leads, I learned that over 50 percent of the *sales professionals* said that referrals are the best source. Everyone seems to know this, but does the company have a strategy to generate referral leads?

The majority of companies I am familiar with do not have a written, thought out plan for lead generation or lead management. If a lead is generated, then there has to be a well thought out process for managing that lead efficiently.

A company should shoulder most of the responsibility for lead generation. A *sales professional's* time is too limited and valuable to have most of the responsibility for lead generation. It should be the company's job to develop and facilitate lead generation, not only external but also internal. Companies need to strategize and have a well thought out plan for lead generation. They need to educate, inform and train others in the company on their responsibilities concerning leads. They must develop a process for employees to generate and qualify leads and to ensure that this information gets passed to the appropriate person for handling.

Companies have to remember and teach that "Everyone is in sales"! Remember, this idea as well as others are *threaded* through all the **SSC** stages, once you learn a proven idea, strategy or technique, use it everywhere you can!

Let The Prospecting Begin:

Drop By Cold Calls

I have found that just walking into a prospect's office location and expecting to talk to a decision maker is a very *low percentage move*. Many times, a *gatekeeper* will say they will give any information to the person responsible and I can watch my door to any opportunity close.

There have been occasions when the decision maker just happened to be at the front desk, and this is where being prepared is a must. You have to have a quick value proposition of why this person should take the time to listen to your "*spiel*". My definition of a *spiel* is a pre-planned and pre-thought out overview of the benefits of using your company's products and services. Being ready with letters of recommendation to hand the prospect helps build credibility. At such times, I always stress that I appreciate their time and was just going to drop off the letters of recommendation and business card; and then, if they were interested, I had planned to set up a meeting at a later date. I have received fairly good response with this *approach* because I was respecting their time and didn't expect a meeting without a prior agreement.

Route Sales

As with everything, there are exceptions, route sales, for example. In route sales many times companies are used to having *sales professionals* drop by unannounced. I did route sales at two of the companies where I worked. I did not deliver any products; I was the liaison from our company on new promotions and products. I sold products, promotions and helped ensure full products selection, including the best shelf and floor locations.

At Warner Lambert, I had a list of 120 accounts that I called on monthly. I was only allowed to have a maximum of 120 accounts in my assigned territory; but I could add and drop accounts, so that I had the top accounts on my list. If I found a new store, I would drop by to talk to the department head and introduce myself and my company. Warner Lambert had several leading products: Listerine, Benadryl, Sinutab and Efferdent, so it gave me some initial creditability. It was just part of the department head's day to keep abreast of what was new to help their department be more profitable. There is an important distinction here. You can sell large volumes of retail items to consumers; but, it is the store selling to the consumer, not a B2B *sales professional* selling to each consumer. We were selling to the stores that, in turn, sold to the consumer.

I would ask my new prospect if they had a few minutes. If they said yes, I would thank them and then go into my update on our latest promotions. When I finished, I would ask for a good day, time or time frame to stop by the next month. Even if they said it didn't matter, I would tell them I knew they are very busy and there must be certain days and times that would be better for me to stop by each month. This tactic worked well and I used it successfully while working at both Warner Lambert and Trend/West Coast.

This technique worked out fairly well for route sales. You get better quality selling time and you are acknowledging their time is valuable.

When it comes to B2B sales, excluding route type sales, dropping by unannounced and cold calling prospects is a *low percentage move.*

It might have worked in the past, but in today's "Information Age" decision makers are on information overload and solicitation overload. Companies have to remember that as the *environment* changes, so do your strategies and techniques.

However, if you arrive in a town or area early for an appointment, if you finish an appointment early or if the contact has left word that she will be quite late, it never hurts to cold call any prospects in the area. Furthermore, if you will be traveling far to meet a contact with an appointment, it is always a good idea to call his competitors nearby before you travel, to see if you can get an appointment with them while you are in the area. An interesting tactic is to say that you will be visiting XYZ Company and was wondering if ABC Company had a few minutes to talk, also. The cold call recipient may wonder why his competitor has agreed to an appointment with you and just may grant you one with him as well. See more on this tactic under *lily padding*.

I have worked for many companies that never quite figured out they were making a BIG MISTAKE.

For example, while working for Kinko's, I did some walk-in cold calling. This activity was not by my choice but mandated by the top sales management. On one campaign, Kinko's wanted to let companies know that we now had the capability to make banners and signs. Accordingly, they had the branch manager and I go door-to-door cold calling in the local downtown area. We found out that some retail stores might do a couple of vinyl banners a year using Kinko's new capabilities. Now, let's do the numbers. Kinko's had three standard sizes: $53 for a small banner, $84 for a medium one and $105 for a large banner. One of my personal monthly goals was approximately $50,000 in sales and I was also responsible for helping the branch make its monthly goal. Since I had to sell $2,500 per day to make my individual goal, how many banners would I have to sell each day of cold calling?

Per day quota - $2,500 per day, figuring average of 20 selling days per month, $50,000 per month.

Small vinyl banners - 48 per day, 944 monthly

Medium vinyl banners - 30 per day, 596 monthly

Large vinyl banners - 24 per day, 476 monthly

If you add in the branch manager's salary, how many would we have had to sell? The answer is a lot! We had several retailers interested and two told us it was nice to know; but we only sold a few banners the day the branch manager and I did the sales blitz.

We then had a conference call to talk about the results. Most of the teams had the same results as my branch manager and I did, yet the top sales management was ecstatic with the results.

From this experience, we can see that the first mistake is not figuring out how much you have to sell to make a profit. The second huge mistake is not taking into consideration the total potential of the targeted prospective customers. As a B2B *sales professional*, I always had to be thinking of a portfolio of customers that would help ensure I would reach my monthly and yearly quotas. I would have never chosen to prospect retail stores in the downtown area. On earlier occasions, many *sales professionals* in Kinko's had "Evaluated and Eliminated" these companies for not having the total yearly business to make it onto our portfolio list. We were allowed to have only 40 businesses on our account lists, and we made sure that those 40 were the best to help ensure reaching our goals and making the most commissions.

Did Kinko's want small downtown retail stores' business? Yes, but they should have been approached using another lower *cost of acquisition* strategy. Mailing coupons announcing the banners as new products or sending lower-cost employees to blitz the downtown area by handing out fliers and coupons for banners would have been a much better use of our company's resources. Notice I said using mail with coupons. This is not the same as letters to decision makers from the sales force looking to gain an appointment.

Another example of where Kinko's forgot to "do the numbers" is when we were heading into the holiday season. The retail side of Kinko's, the store locations, would have retail promotions on holiday items such as personalized calendars, holiday cards and, in this particular year, personalized Christmas tree ornaments, which retailed for $5.50 each.

Just like with the launch of banners and signs, we had a sales and management teleconference for all the branches in the inland northwest to talk about these holiday promotions. The top sales management announced a contest for the branches. The management of the branches who could sell the most holiday items would get monetary prizes. Again, let's do the numbers. Two examples were the highest priced of the promotion items: personalized calendars for $19.95 each with coupon and the lowest which was a Christmas tree ornament selling for $5.50. How many would I have to sell to make my numbers?

Per day quota - $2,500 per day, figuring average of 20 selling days per month, $50,000 per month.

Calendars - 126 per day - 2,507 monthly

Ornaments - 455 per day - 9,091 monthly

Again, Kinko's top sales management was making several mistakes with these sales *approaches*. They were not "doing the numbers", confusing B2B – business-to-business sales with B2C – business-to-consumer sales and focusing on a one-time sale, *project* vs. a *program*. The lesson here is that companies have to be *aware* of the *cost of acquisition* for many of its customers. When using B2B sales forces to sell to B2C prospects, companies will lose money in the majority of cases.

My branch won the holiday contest. We were the number one branch in the district, which included four different western states. Cold calls were not mandated this time, just strongly recommended. Top management recommended sales blitzes on holiday promotions just as they had done before on the banners. I did not do one single cold call. How did I help lead our branch to win the contest? As I stated before, the **SSC** stages blend together but have to be studied separately to better understand, so I will finish this success story in the **Closing Strategy stage**.

Another recent example is at a weekly company meeting for the two companies I represent now. One of the managers thought it would be a good idea to go around the room and ask everyone to think of a lead for the marketing and sales department. Most of the leads were not what we, the marketing and sales department, would consider our B2B *target audience*.

At the next weekly meeting I brought in some interesting figures. Our department "did the numbers" and looked at existing customers compared to the ones given to us as leads in the previous meeting. We took the last three years' business from each example and figured out the monthly average of business for each existing customer. Then, we figured out how many of this type of customer would it take to make Sales' monthly goal if we had no other existing customers. We categorized them using our A, B, C, D, type of customers. Again, we were assuming we had no other customers but had to rely on the number of customer in each example to reach our goal. The result shocked even me.

A customer: #1 - 5 of this type of customer

A customer: #2 - 17 of this type of customer

B customer: #1 - 30 of this type of customer

B customer: #2 - 83 of this type of customer

C customer: #1 - 192 of this type of customer

C customer #2: - 259 of this type of customer

D customer #1: - 600 of this type of customer

D customer #1: - 725 of this type of customer

E-Z customer #1: - 5,190 of this type of customer

E-Z customer #2: - 24,194 of this type of customer

Almost all of the leads given to the sales and marketing department were the E-Z examples. Now, if you consider the cost of supporting the number of customers in the last two examples, you find it is near impossible. We had been in business for over 14 years and our total customer base was not even half of the last example, 24,194, of that particular type customer to reach our goal.

This is why it is in a company's best interest to set up a maximum amount of customers that each B2B sales person on their sales force can have in his or her portfolio. At Warner Lambert it was 120 and, at another company I worked for, it was 50. This helps the sales force understand that they will have to focus on a type of customer that will help them make their quota.

If there were five keys to a company's success, truly understanding "doing the numbers" would be one of them. Companies and their sales forces have to focus their time on a *target audience* that is manageable long term.

KEY TAKEAWAY

Sales is a numbers game, so don't forget to do the numbers.

Setup and Approach

Your investigation and preplanning is key to setting up a strategy for "increasing your odds" to secure an appointment. The first step is to gain *intelligence,* so you can use my "Turn a cold call into a *warm call*" technique. This information will substantially *increase your odds* of gaining an appointment.

You have to become a "PI", private investigator. Do you or anyone inside or outside of your company know someone in the targeted prospect company? This is a hugely important step to your success. I have talked to others in my company and gotten a name of a medium level contact. This is usually not the decision maker but someone who would be a *warm call* to help me in my *intelligence* investigation of the company. I am amazed at how many times I have taken a little bit of time and found a contact name in a prospective account. I would call the contact, introduce myself and tell them who gave me their name; and in a majority of times, I received a positive reaction. For example, "Garth told me that you would be a great person to help me find out who to give a quick call, so I could give that person a update on how we have been helping ABC company this last year. By the way, Garth said to tell you hi." I also tell them that I am a very user friendly salesman and they usually laugh. Remember, you are NOT trying to sell this person your products or services. Your goal is to gain valuable information to help you formulate your *approach.* Many times, the person has given me important information, such as the name of the decision maker and problems the company has been having that could benefit from my company's services. Sometimes, I learn that they are using a competitor; sometimes they will even tell me things their company likes or dislikes about my competitor. This type of upfront investigation can help substantially *increase your odds* of gaining an appointment and a sale. Pieces of key information, such as who is their present vendor, help you strategize the *next steps* in your *approach.*

KEY TAKEAWAY

The setup and approach is a key to "increasing your odds" in prospecting!

I also ask the contact if I can use their name when calling the person they recommend. Remember, always try to make all cold calls into *warm calls.* I get the contact's vital information, direct phone number, title, and length of time with the company, etc. Another critical thing this technique accomplishes is it gets me around the *gatekeeper*.

I have heard some senior people in sales management tell the *sales professional* to do some investigation before making the phone call, but the right type of information was not discussed. The information that they wanted was not the most beneficial to getting an appointment or even very helpful in an initial sales call. They have wanted the sales force to go to the prospective company's website and gather a broad range of information. Remember, your goal is to get an appointment, not to sell your products or services before the appropriate time.

As stated before, in the MMA competition, kicking and specifically head kicks are now successful because of proper *set up*. Gathering a bunch of financial information about the company's last two quarters and who is on the board of directors is not always the key information in securing an appointment with a decision maker.

KEY TAKEAWAY

Knowing about a company makes you knowledgeable. Knowing about a customer's problems and how to help them makes you valuable.

Having key pieces of information before you call the decision maker, you can structure your *approach* and have a contact name as a referral. Now, the prospecting call is somewhat of a *warm call* and not a total cold call. Remember, one of the *sales professional's* top goals in prospecting is always to try to *warm call* and not to cold call. This is one of the most important keys in successful prospecting.

KEY TAKEAWAY

In prospecting, one of the top goals is to turn every cold call into a warm call!

The time spent investigating up front to help you in your *approach* becomes shorter and shorter with experience; but remember that you are not writing your thesis on the prospect. You are only trying to gain enough information to help *increase your odds* of securing an appointment. The bigger the opportunity, the more up-front time you will put into your *approach*.

Let's stop for a second. Notice that I am presenting strategies and techniques that I have used successfully in today's ultra-competitive environment. They are not a group of theories that have never been tested in a realistic environment. On the contrary, I have discovered *Truths* and *Universal Truths*. Learn from them, but remember that nobody is the *Holder of the Truth* and nobody knows it all.

Companies need to encourage *sales professionals* to exchange successful strategies and techniques freely with the entire sales force. I have been asked by other *sales professionals* for advice on sales strategies and techniques, but I have worked for only one company where the sales management asked me or any of the other *sales professional* to share successful strategies or techniques on an on-going basis. At Warner Lambert, our sales team was at the top or near the top of the performance list for the entire country month after month, and my sales manager for Washington State encouraged the entire sales team to share any successful techniques or strategies to increase sales. Our sales manager would then forward voice mails weekly of any and all new ideas.

The other companies I worked for should have followed the same approach of encouraging the exchanging of successful sales strategies and techniques. After all these years, it amazes me that only now are large studies beginning to discover that this single technique dramatically increases companies' sales. This tactic was considered just common sense beginning with my first sales position out of college.

Times, Days and Ways to Start Calling

From years in sales, I have determined certain times and days that I feel are best for calling prospects on the phone. Through my research, I have also found that many sales experts agree with me that these optimal times will *increase your odds* of success.

I make the majority of my prospecting phone calls and *follow up* calls on Tuesdays and Thursdays. If there is an overflow, I use Wednesdays. Mondays and Fridays are saved for calling existing customers for attempting to increase sales or whatever reason is necessary.

My logic is that Mondays are the start of the week when many people are less open to a prospecting call, even a "Warm" prospecting call. On Fridays, customers are generally trying to wrap up the week's business prior to the weekend.

I usually wait until 9:00am before my first prospecting call. I will not start at 8:00am sharp, as I feel that many customers will not be most receptive to a sales call as their first call in the morning. However,

I will return a call early in the morning to answer a customer's question and to demonstrate a quick response. My prospecting calls end after 4:00pm, I feel many prospects are starting to focus on wrapping things up for the day.

Also, I start my calls off on a positive note by calling an existing customer and thanking them for their business or by calling back a customer who has already committed that they want to start working with our company. This strategy has allowed me to start my calling with a positive mindset.

Another personal but important note is that I try to make my calls from a place that will be free of interruptions. Once you get into a positive calling rhythm, you do not want to be interrupted, as interruptions will reduce the number of quality prospecting calls you make and the quality of the calls. Studies find that over 50 percent of communication is non-verbal, body communication. Consequently, you are at a disadvantage on the phone, and you are intently focusing on the goal of getting an appointment. You are selling the benefit of the appointment and being interrupted or distracted just lessens your chances for success.

Another key to increasing your odds is a technique that I have used for a while. When calling prospects that I hope will call me back, I leave my cellular phone number so I will be available, especially on the day I call. I will take my cellular with me everywhere, just in case the prospect should call back. As a result, I receive a number of calls during the lunch hours. Nothing reduces your odds more than prospects playing phone tag with you when returning your call. If you do miss a call, then call them back and have to leave another message, make sure to apologize for the phone tag. Then, ask that they please try again and leave the best times to call you back. Your goal is to avoid the phone tag, to be available and not to miss the call, which might be the only time the prospect calls you back.

Many sales experts will recommend setting the bar high for numbers of calls. If you think you can make 50 a day, shoot for 100. I strongly disagree. Their logic is that it's a numbers game. That is the only part on which I agree. Sales is a numbers game, but "Avoid Playing the Lottery". The goal of any company or sales manager should be how many appointments did their *sales professionals* get. To be more precise, how many quality appointments did they get? Do the appointments have potential to be an A, B or C account? That should be the true gauge of success.

I was reading an article by Jill Konrath of SellingToBigCompanies. com. She mentioned a past sales manager asking her how many prospecting calls she made the week before. She hated to lie; but, to not get herself into trouble, she played the game. I have had the same situation several times during my sales career. Some sales managers wanted me to "Play the Game", which is a code phrase for lying. I suspected that the sales manager's main focus was filling in his reports and not getting into trouble. On a few occasions, I have told my managers the truth and was then told to make a bunch of calls, even if they were unproductive. Jill Konrath and I were both having good results with what we were doing, getting quality appointments and closing deals; but the sales manager's only goal was to do things the way he/she had been trained.

"Working smarter and not harder" is a key to getting more appointments. Quality appointments should be sought first, and then followed by quantity. Many companies require *sales professionals* to make 100 unproductive *low percentage* calls, when making 20 quality calls to the right type of customers will do much more to promote successful sales.

> **KEY TAKEAWAY**
>
> **The true gauge of successful prospecting is the number of appointments, <u>not</u> number of phone calls.**

The next step is to phone the key contact. Again, I have not had that much success with sending an introductory letter before my call, so I skip it. Instead, I have received good results by forwarding letters of recommendation, a business card and a handwritten note before my call. With the information that you have gathered, you now can strategize and pre-plan your phone call. Your phone conversation needs to be short, succinct, and offer benefits for why it is in the prospect's best interest to give you their valuable time for an appointment. If it is a large opportunity, many times I mentally predict the objection, "I just do not have the time right now" and, as part of my story, pitch or *spiel*, I offer to take the prospect to lunch so as not to take time out of their busy schedule. (Notice that taking the prospect out to lunch is the same technique I used in the **Retention Strategy stage**.)

Make a quick reference to the person who referred them, mention you would like to get together for a quick meeting to tell them how you have helped XYZ (insert the name of a company or companies that they will recognize) with the challenges they faced. The challenges should be the same ones that your initial contact gave to you. Also, stress that the other companies are now very happy that they spent a little time with you. You may mention that a couple of them did not have an immediate need, but some have called you back after you met with them and have told you that they now have an immediate problem and are glad they took the time to meet with you. If you are successful and the prospect agrees to go to lunch with you, it is similar to but not the same as the time you spend with an existing customer.

With an existing customer, you are trying to build on an existing relationship. In prospecting, it is not just going to lunch. You have to keep the conversation light and try to build trust and the start of a relationship. Try to keep it light, even if the prospect brings up business. Be concise and to the point. This is not the place for a big sales pitch.

What if the prospect tells you they don't even have time for lunch? You better be ready with a *talk off* to handle the objection.

As in any martial arts competition, you always have to have plan A, B and C. You go for move A and the opponent reacts or resists differently to A. You already have move B ready, expecting that the first move A, might not work. Many times, I go for move B and he reacts again. I then go back to move A. Sometimes, I go for A to B then to C, then back to A.

Senior Grandmaster Ed Parker was famous for his creation and use of terminology to help better teach physical motion. One of his many terms was the "Equation Formula", which stated:

> *To any given base, you can prefix, suffix, insert, rearrange, alter, adjust, regulate, and delete ideas and moves.*

The same is true in the sales world. *Sales professionals* would do well to learn the "Equation Formula" for sales. You have to have a *base* move but always have alternatives as the situation changes. If you call for an appointment and they tell you they do not have time or are not interested, you have to be able to make adjustments. Many of the objections are just like those in the martial arts world. Most of the time, if you go for one move, there are only a handful of situations that are likely to come about. Companies and sales managers have to "arm" their sales force with the *base* technique and then teach the "Equation

Formula" to better handle objections.

One of the most common objections is that they just do not have the time now, not even for lunch but to call them back in a couple of weeks. This is another critical step in prospecting. "Always keep the Ball in Your Court"! Always offer to call the prospect back. Do not tell them to give you a call back when it slows down or they are not busy. In this business environment, prospects will always be busy and you will never get a return call if you leave it up to them. Always be the one who calls back. By doing so, you remain in control. "Hey, I will give you a call back in three weeks. By then you will be well through your year's end". I then make notes of any key details that might help me resell the benefits of our having a meeting. For instance, if he mentioned that he really would like to meet, I put this in my notes in my CRM system, so that it will give me a positive mind set when I call him back. Great *follow up* is the difference between a good sales person and a great sales person. To have great *follow up* you need a CRM system of some type.

When you call the prospect back in three weeks, just as you said you would, you will be reminded by your CRM system. Before the call, review your notes; if they said to call them back, mention you are calling them back to set up a meeting as they had requested. Also, mention anything else new that can help resell the benefits of meeting with you.

KEY TAKEAWAY
Always keep the ball in your court!

If the prospect tells you that she just does not have the time or is happy with her current vendor, you need to have pre-set *talk offs* to overcome these objections. Again, having *intelligence,* such as knowing whom they use allows you to formulate your moves before you call the main contact.

A response might be that a customer of yours, ABC Company, liked their last vendor also but thought that your company's service was superior at a lower rate. Knowing in advance who they use will help you be prepared to overcome the objection. I have been called "pleasantly persistent" by some prospects. My goal is to maintain a constant balance and not to cross the line by being seen as pushy.

Some prospects test salespeople to see if they really are interested in the prospect's account. Pleasant persistence can show them that you care now and that you will care later, when they are an account and need your help. Often, you are selling you and your future treatment of the future customer.

Another response I will use, "Many of our clients have been loyal to our company for years, and we really respect that. However, situations change quickly, so may I call you back in a couple of months, just to touch bases?" Most will say that is agreeable. Remember the "Ball is Still in My Court". I also tell them I will forward them letters of recommendation so they will know how we have helped other companies like theirs. I will send two to three specific letters of recommendation from companies in similar industries, especially if one of the references has used the competitor that this prospect currently uses. I also send a one page overview of my company. If the recommendation letters build interest, then the one page company overview gives them a concise indication of our strengths. If I know who the competitor is that they use, I make minor changes to stress our strong points over that particular competitor.

No Thanks!

Another situation is when the prospect tells you "No thanks", either nicely or abruptly. This has happened to anyone who has been in sales for any time at all. I like to remember the following quote when I have a streak of rejection.

KEY TAKEAWAY

"Never let the fear of striking out get in your way."

Babe Ruth, baseball great

What should a *sales professional* do when confronted with a strong negative? First, remember that things change quickly in today's business world. There could be a *change in guard* with this particular prospect. If this prospect has big potential, I would schedule a call back or a drop by in my CRM system to see if anything has changed. At a later date, I may learn that there has been a *change in guard.* Then, I will make another try on that prospect company; but this time, I will attempt to accumulate a little more *intelligence* on the prospect.

If the prospect gives you a firm "No thanks!" it is also the time to do a *post-call* review to think over quickly what I have said. Could I have said it differently, better or both? I do not beat myself up over a strong negative. Instead, I just learn from it, whether it is in the mixed martial arts or *mixed selling arts* world.

> **KEY TAKEAWAY**
> **The biggest mistake isn't making a mistake but not learning from it to improve.**

These techniques are models of what I mean when I say *sophisticated basics* or *advanced basics*. I am calling the prospect and asking for an appointment. That prospecting technique has been around since the phone was invented. What I have done over the years is "tighten up the gaps" by continually tightening and improving my technique.

The same applies when I am grappling. I am doing the same moves that have been around for years but just making them more and more effective. When teaching grappling seminars, I have a saying that many of the students who have attended my earlier seminars know the answer before I finish. Where do you lose opponents? Many yell out "In transitions!" The point is that if your moves are loose with poor *follow up* and lots of gaps, your opponent will escape your grasp. In the *mixed selling arts* world, the *basics* are the same. I have merely *sophisticated and tightened up the basics*, rather than using more complexity with complicated sophistication. Under pressure, you must always go back to the basics, be it in martial or in sales.

A perfect example of this thinking was in an email that Mark Clark, my former boss at Collection Bureau and Account Billing Service sent out to the team leaders:

> *"The company baseball team has given me an insight. We are getting a return on our investment. Now for the insight.*
>
> *Steve, one of the team's pitchers, told me that the pitching mound at the field where the team has been practicing is ten feet closer to the batter than the regulation field. He said that he had become used to pitching at that shorter distance; and, then when there was a game and he had to pitch 10 feet further, it made a big difference. He explained that with that small difference the angles of pitching change significantly.*
>
> *This made me think about the theory that very small changes can have a substantial effect on results. If you can follow this at all, I would like the team leaders to think about what little changes they can implement in their departments that will drastically increase the results (billing, collections and sales). Let me know your thoughts. Thanks Mark."*

73

Mark Clark was right on track. This is an ideal illustration of *sophisticated basics*. The playing field, first base through home plate, pitchers mound, bats, and balls have not changed. The framework of the game is the same; but because the *environment* has changed small refinements of the *basics* have to be made to have the best chance for success.

I always stress to keep going back to the basics. This means the *core moves*, the techniques that have been around for years, are time tested and are *Universal Truths*. *Core moves* need to be constantly refined and improved. Telephone prospecting has been used for decades. It is a *basic, core* prospecting tool. The key is continually to find new ways to utilize the phone more efficiently. Nowadays, prospecting through emails has become a *core move* as a prospecting tool. Accordingly, it is essential to refine and improve continually the way emails are used to prospect, as well as all other prospecting tools and techniques.

Top Down Selling Always The Best?

There has been much talk about "top down" selling and many books have been written about it. All of them preach that anything else is a waste of valuable sales time; and if a high level executive were to say that his company should use your company's products and/or services, then there is a high probability that your company would be in first place to help the prospective company with their needs. Many of these experts and authors say to go high and then get pushed down to the next levels. On the contrary, I say you stand a high probability of getting pushed out of the opportunity. Selling high is different than prospecting high.

If a mixed martial arts competitor were trying to be the next champion, they would have to earn their opportunity. They could not just call up the champion and challenge them to a title shot, without experience or a good record. It is the same in sales. It is not always the best strategy to try to meet a CXO, president or high-level executive in your first prospecting meeting with a new company.

Many times, I have asked who the decision maker for my type of products and services was and I have been told the administrator or CXO. When this happened, I have gone to the middle management first. I have contacted them and told them that I have other clients (naming a few who most likely will be recognized) and that they have told me they are just bombarded with marketing and sales people. Could I set up a quick meeting with them to discuss how we help other customers; and, again, I quickly name them. I promise them that I will make sure to provide a piece of information that they will be able to use. If they think our products and services might be worth a meeting with the administrator/CXO level, then they can help set that up. This is another technique that has worked several times for me. It is a tactic that I keep in my tool kit for when the time arises.

If I have an inside track to get an appointment with a high level executive, then, of course, I will start prospecting there. Higher is better; but, remember that, getting in is better than not getting in at all.

A study showed that over 50 percent of sales professionals do not locate, reach, and contact the correct decision makers. Many times, finding an easy way into the prospective account is a logical first step. Here is a note to sales managers and *sales professionals*: Many top level management people really do not care or do not have time to get involved in every purchasing decision of their company. They rely on others in the company either to make the decisions or to find vendors; and then the higher up management just gives their token approval.

When I was with Kinko's, I worked with a customer's mid-level employee on several *projects*. I always asked him what was the goal of each *project*. On one particular *project*, the contact told me he was going to do several test jobs: I worked closely with him on the first few jobs and I used an *order starter* originally to get my foot in the door with this particular contact. More on what an *order starter* is will be covered in more depth in the **Closing Strategy stage**, but the goal for this *project* was to roll it out across the country to all 1,400 plus of his company's locations. Wow! I worked closely with this mid-level contact for months. Finally, he told me it was time to start looking at the final job. I asked him the specifics, timelines and if anyone besides him had to approve the job before I had it run. I told him I would make sure we had all the resources and manpower to meet his deadlines, but I would need a signed commitment from his company. He gave me the name of a vice president in the company. I told him he needed to help me set up a meeting with that vice president and that I would go to my branch manager to confirm that we could meet his deadline. I also said that our ultimate goal was to make him look good.

Selling "top down" isn't always the best strategy. The vice president, a very nice woman, had no interest in the fact that I had been helping my contact out with numerous *projects* for the last several of months. Her sole concern was that the contact sponsor had trust in me and my company and that I could get the job done in the time frame they needed. Although, price wasn't a factor, I did give them our volume discount. The vice president totally trusted the middle level contact and me to get the job done. She was just the "token" signature for a job with a very high price tag. On a day-to-day basis, she would have never gotten involved with my company or me.

Note: never gouge a customer. Get paid for your total value, but never gouge. I have been very successful in taking away business from a competitor who was gouging a customer just because they were loyal and never checked.

Mark Clark, my former boss at Collection Bureau, Inc. and Account Billing Service, received hundreds of calls every week. If you were a sales professional and called into his voice mail, you would have had a better chance buying a lottery ticket than meeting with him.

Several studies' findings just reinforced my strategies over the years. The studies concluded that in order to increase your chances substantially of getting an appointment with a top executive, you had to have been recommended by someone inside the company, you needed a strong relationship with the person and you had to have a proven track record. Other similar studies have also found that the main reason a high-level executive will meet with a *sales professional* is based on existing relationships from fellow business associates inside or outside of the company. These relationships were the highest predictor of whether the prospect would agree to meet with sales *professionals*.

That is why I have had good success at finding an easy way into a prospective company. Once in the door, I go on a reconnaissance mission to find the *intelligence* to *set up* my *approach* to the best contact for my products and services.

KEY TAKEAWAY
Selling to the top is different from prospecting to the top.

High Percentage Prospecting Techniques:

Using a Subject Expert

Many companies' offerings are becoming more complex; and, consequently, experts are becoming more and more necessary in every step of the sales process. Prospecting is no exception. *Sales professionals* often need internal support.

While working at ITG, sometimes I would offer my "Quick Update" technique to a prospect, combined with offering to bring in a subject expert. We had some of the most knowledgeable IT subject experts in the northwest. If the prospect appeared to have good potential, I would offer to bring a subject expert along with me on the initial sales appointment as an added value or enticement. This strategy worked because even if the person I was talking to didn't have or see an immediate need, they would bring in a manager from another department who would be interested in talking with our subject expert. Using this strategy secured me many appointments that I might not have gotten without the added enticement.

Of course, companies and sales forces have to understand this makes the cost of an appointment substantially higher, given the *sales professional's* and the subject expert's time. One has to be very selective when bringing along a company's experts to a sales call. Most companies have a very limited amount of subject experts; and therefore, *sales professionals* have to be diligent in getting the most out of the company's limited resources. Fortunately, the Internet is and has become another tool or *"core move"* that can be utilized to bring a subject expert to a prospect or customer. The use of online conferencing is a great way to bring a subject expert to a sales situation at a very low cost.

"Just want to give you a quick update"

As mentioned previously, a technique I used when I worked for Kinko's was to check to see if I could find a contact to call, usually an administrative assistant. I would use my *"Just want to give you a quick update"* technique and tell them I was told that they would be a key contact for our company. They loved the feeling of being important and getting to meet some of the company's representatives. I did this over and over again to get my foot in the door. This tactic enables me to gather valuable information about key contacts, decision makers, etc. Also, I could sell through to the administrative levels, because even if the high level managers were the ones who signed off on a $1,000.00 plus order, the administrative assistant was the unofficial decision maker. Once you earned an administrative assistant's trust, he or she would help you get to other key decision makers. Many times, the administrative assistants are the *gatekeepers*, and now you have the *gatekeeper* as your ally. Sometimes, using this approach, I would pick up small *projects*, earn trust and turn them into *programs*, which was my goal.

It has been my experience that the people at the administrative assistant level are some of the hardest working people in a company. Generally, they have a great deal of work and pressure with little recognition or pay. A *sales professional* treating them with respect and giving them the attention they deserve, goes a long way to building a productive relationship. They often become an ally and sponsor for larger opportunities. Because you have developed a channel to inside, internal *intelligence* to help you find the right contact for larger opportunities, you are less likely to be one of the over 50 percent of *sales professionals* who fail to make contact with a decision maker.

However, there is a <u>but</u> to this technique. If the lower level person has an existing relationship with another vendor, then you will have to go over the person's head or around them. This tactic can burn the relationship with the entry-level contact; but if you aren't getting anywhere with them, then you have less to lose by going over their head.

I have used the technique of going over the initial contact's head several times. I have used it when I have exhausted all the attempts with the lower to mid-level contacts. You might ask why I didn't just go to the top at the beginning. As I mentioned before, I try to use *high percentage moves* because there are no perfect moves.

With new prospects, many times it is difficult or nearly impossible to get an appointment with a CXO without having had previous sales success in the company. Sometimes *sales professionals* will have to ask executives in their companies to make phone calls to help establish an appointment. At such times, I may bring in the owners of my company to help secure the appointment. The principals of my company are willing to assist in a limited amount of prospecting.

An executive level person of one company will have a better chance of receiving a call back from another company's executive than a *sales professional* will, but executives, presidents and owners usually do not want to be sales people. However, at times it is necessary for them to get involved to secure an appointment, and they need to remember that everyone in the company is in sales!

Combination Site Visit and Phone Call

One of my favorite *high percentage techniques* for prospecting which I have developed in the last few years is a combination of a site visit and then a *follow up* phone call to gain an appointment. If I do not have any *intelligence* about the prospect, before I place a call, I will drop by the prospect's office armed with references and/or letters of recommendation from other companies they might recognize.

This is when you get to use the reference letters that you worked so hard for in the **Retention stage**.

Since the front desk people generally are *gatekeepers*, I will pick up a business card and then ask the name of the person in charge of the services that my company offers. I will quickly add that I only want to leave some information and letters of recommendation for the decision maker. This approach works often, because I do not appear to be pushy. By saying that I only want to leave some information, the front desk person usually will lower their guard. I am not trying to talk to the potential contact, which would seem pushy by not respecting their time and expecting a meeting uninvited. No, I just want to leave some references from other clients like themselves that demonstrate how we have helped their businesses.

I usually have three letters of recommendation and my business card on top. I print all my letters of recommendation on very nice resume paper, so they look like impressive originals. Also, I include a one-page overview of my company and a list of our services as the last page. Now is the time to ask for the contact's name, correct spelling and official title. I have a prepared yellow sticky that I complete by writing the name of the contact. The sticky says something like, "I would love to help you out as we have with these clients." It is all handwritten to achieve a personal touch. Then, I give the information to the front desk person and I ask if anyone is working with them now. Sometimes, because I appear to be less threatening by only wanting to drop off information, they will tell me if they use a competitor, the competitor's name and if they are happy with them or not. All this intelligence now can be used to formulate my *talk off* when I call for an appointment. Score!

Then I go back and enter the information into my CRM system to *follow up* the next week with a phone call. Now that I have more *intelligence*, I can strategize my *setup* and *approach*. Remember, *strategize* is a code word for "the art of carefully planning towards a specific goal." Armed with the contact's name, title and whether they are using another vendor, I have turned a future cold call into a *warm call*. I have warmed it up with a "pre-call touch" as one of my favorite sales experts, Dave Kahle of The DaCo Corporation, would refer to it. Also, since I have been to the prospect's location and dropped off letters of references, when I do make my call, it will not be like a typical cold call.

Now that I have a name and company, I can do a quick last check. Does anyone in my company know this person or company? Do I have other customers who might know them? Usually not, but it's worth a last quick check, to "Increase My Odds".

As mentioned previously, I try to call the prospects on certain days and times, hopefully during the prospects' less busy or crazy times. When I call in, I ask for the contact by first name. If there is any hesitation, maybe there is more than one Cindy for example, then I give the last name.

These are subtle techniques that I have developed over years of prospecting. If you call in and ask for the CXO, administrator, office manager, Mrs. Cindy Doe, or person in charge of X department, you will most likely alert the *gatekeeper* to have their guard up. Then you run the risk of the *gatekeeper*'s asking, "What it is pertaining to?" If I have an inside or outside contact, I will say that I was referred by my contact, using their name and company's name, to give her a quick call. If I don't have a name to use, then I would tell them I am calling regarding the reference letters I forwarded to the prospective contact.

If you make it through to the prospective contact, you better have planned what you are going to say before you say it. I have been doing prospecting for over 20 years and I still rehearse at least mentally what I am going to say, a *talk off*.

If I had another company that even remotely knew this company, then I would say that they had mentioned that it might be a good idea to call them because the businesses' challenges are similar and we have really helped their company. However, if I have no one referring me, then I ask if they received the letters of recommendation. I mention that my company's services have really helped out the companies that I provided letters from. This is also a good time to mention that some of the companies told us that we provide superior services to any of their past vendors and that they are glad they found us. Now, it is time for my "*Just want to give you a quick update*" technique. Remember, my current goal is to get an appointment, so it is important here to sell the value of the appointment and NOT to give a sales pitch on products and services.

Of course, just as the martial arts are not a perfect science, neither are the *mixed selling arts*. If pressed, and they start asking questions about your company's products and services, you had better use planned responses or *talk offs*. If you found out that they use one of your competitors, then you will have crafted your discussion around your strengths and the competitor's weaknesses. You do not even need to mention the competitor's name. A long-standing rule in sales is not to talk badly about the competition.

Remote Prospecting

I have closed many new customers on the telephone without ever meeting them in person.

I use the same basic technique for remote prospects: I call and ask for the person who handles the service and/or product I sell, quickly tell them I am going to send them a letter and I would like to get their name spelled correctly. I also ask for their official title. Typically, they will give me both, because I am not trying to have a lengthy conversation with them. A little refinement that I used is the Internet. If you Google the company, the person's name, title and contact information may be online. I then call to verify the person is still working there. Frequently, the person has gone and the website has not been updated. I then use the same basic techniques. I check for any *intelligence* and mail, fax or email letters of recommendation, a brief letter and an overview of our company. My goal is still to set up an appointment; it will just be with a short phone call instead of in person.

Overall, I have been very successful with this technique and I will continue to use it and improve it by making continual adjustments as dictated by the marketplace.

> **KEY TAKEAWAY**
>
> **A sales professional's first goal is to secure an appointment, NOT to make a sale.**

Lily Pad Technique

This is an idea that I picked up from another Kinko's *sales professional*. I no longer remember the context in which he used it; but it shows again how using the MSA methodology, a model of continual learning, I was able to take the idea and dramatically enhance and expand it.

This concept can be used to develop techniques throughout the **SSC**. It is a way for thinking of how a frog jumps from lily pad to lily pad. One way I use this idea in prospecting is when I am visiting with a prospect or an existing client. I am always looking for another prospect in the same building, the building next door, down the street and on the way to the appointment. Then, just like the frog jumping from lily pad to lily pad, I jump from prospect to prospect, opportunity to opportunity.

Lily padding is a very strong prospecting technique for many reasons. When I am next door, I can drop by another business and tell them I have been visiting one of their neighbors; thus, dropping the original company's name and contact. By *leveraging* that relationship, I can drop off some references and information for whoever receives such information for this second company. Not only can you drop off some references, but if the neighboring business is a good reference, use them too. If their neighbor isn't a good reference or is just a prospect, then tell them you drive pass this business all the time, because you work with other companies around them.

Your time is money and with the cost of gasoline, *lily pad* technique makes the best use of your time. You have already invested the time and money going to visit another contact, so why not fully utilize the time you are in the area? Many times, I have been visiting an existing customer and walk down the hall to prospect another company. Just as important, what a low cost way of eliminating a prospect. Drop by and find out that the prospect is not a fit and eliminate them, thereby saving the cost of another trip.

Additionally, whenever you acquire a new customer, you should prospect in all directions: the business next door, next floor, next building, next street and so on. The costs will be substantially less, since you are already there. You can use the *leverage* of your existing new relationship as well as the previous one, i.e., with letters of recommendation.

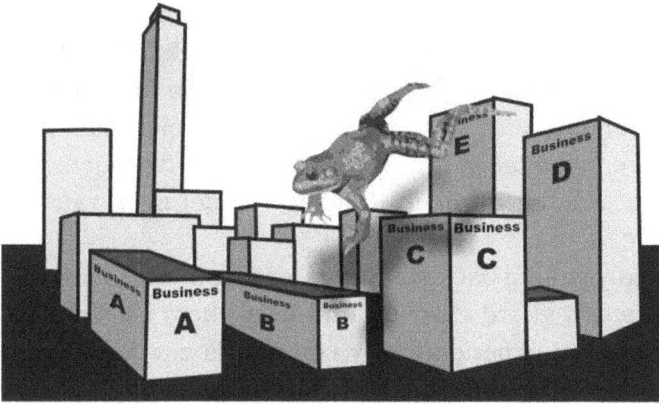

Lily Pad Technique

A fellow *sales professional* who reports to me asked me how I acquired a couple of new customers. I told her I used the *lily pad* technique at the new business complex. She instantly knew what I meant because we share the same sales methodology and sales language.

Just as Senior Grandmaster Ed Parker was famous for using analogies to convey his concepts and principles, companies and sales managers should use easy analogies to help *sales professionals* remember important ideas and also to promote communication throughout your sales force.

The *lily pad* technique is *threaded* throughout the **SSC** and is a powerful concept to remember for all companies and their sales forces.

Dreaded Voice Mail

Frequently, when a *sales professional* makes a prospecting telephone call, they will be asked "What is this pertaining to?" You are being screened by a *gatekeeper*. If you were referred by another client or person, tell the *gatekeeper* that you are calling them on recommendation from that person. Something like, "Susan Smith, operations manager of ABS Corporation told me to contact your Mr. Jones." This tactic gives you a slightly better chance of talking to the person. Even then you may get the voice mail. When leaving a message, make sure to mention the referral's name and company.

When calling in and being told your contact is not available or in a meeting and would you like their voice mail, it is decision time. Do you want to leave a voice mail or wait and try to contact them again?

I almost always say, "Yes put me through." Why? For several reasons; sometimes the contact actually picks up the phone. Score! Be ready for this possibility. Also, listening to the voice mail message can give you more key *intelligence* or confirms your *intelligence*. Listen for names, titles, cellular number, that the contact is on vacation, out of the office, etc.

Repeatedly calling back but never leaving a voice mail will put any good *gatekeeper*'s guard clear up and keep them on red alert. I know this from personal experience. My company's coworkers who answer our phone lines will tell me that a person keeps calling but never leaves a message. Ninety-nine percent of the time it is an aggressive or new *sales professional* trying to sell me something.

I don't always leave a message, because maybe they really are in a meeting, so I will try a couple more times to get through. My goal is to speak to the contact and sell them on why it is important that we meet. A voice mail is not the medium for selling the appointment; it is where you want to sell a reason for them to call you back.

If the person answering the phone will take a message for the contact, be ready! I generally joke with the person and say, "Oh, you are their voice mail". Many times they laugh and agree. This generally lowers their guard a little bit and warms them up somewhat. I always ask their name before I hang up and thank them by using their name, "Thanks, Sue and have a great day," for example. Then, of course, I add the contact names and the *gatekeeper's* name in my CRM system, furthering my *intelligence*.

If prospective contacts are out of the office for any extended amount of time, I rarely leave a voice mail, because when the prospect gets back in the office, they most likely will be swamped with work and calls to return. There is a high likelihood that any sales type messages will be deleted. Therefore, I will schedule in my CRM system to *follow up* a day or two after they get back, making a note that they had been out of the office.

When I do leave voice mails, I have planned out what I am going to say. I try to keep such messages short, clear and concise while utilizing any *intelligence* I have. "I was recommended to call you by (insert contact) of (insert Company's name)". This approach will *increase your odds* of getting a call back.

Do not leave long messages. Practice before you call to reduce the chance of being cut off half way through your message. Make sure to speak clearly, and leave your name and your phone number at least twice. Nothing is more frustrating than having to play back a message several times to hear who the caller is and their phone number. Such callers have not spoken clearly or slowly enough when leaving their message.

You want to give your prospect a reason to call you back and make it easy for them to do so. When leaving a message, give a phone number where you can be reached, either landline or a cellular phone. If I am making prospecting telephone calls, I will leave my cellular phone number to avoid phone tag.

If the prospect calls you back, answer quickly to avoid their having to leave a voice mail. Not only is it a little inconsiderate to be slow to answer; but you might only get one chance. Don't blow it. After a morning of prospect calling, where I have left several voice mail messages, I will take my cell phone to lunch, so as not to miss a call back. I have picked up numerous callbacks while at lunch, because the prospects have been busy and are returning their calls through the lunch hour.

If you are returning a prospect's call, always tell the *gatekeeper*, "I am returning (insert prospect's name) call." Using his name in your response will increase substantially your odds of getting through to the contact.

Following the MSA methodology, I was reading an article by Jeffrey Gitomer, a top selling sales author at www.gitomer.com. He suggested a great technique for getting a prospect's direct line number. When calling in, ask for the prospect's direct voice mail number. I have used this technique and gotten the prospect's direct phone line number for future use. This is just another example of following the MSA methodology and continually learning is just part of the game.

Schedule a Follow Up Call

As mentioned earlier, *follow up* is a key to any *sales professional's* success. If I leave a voice mail or message, I will schedule a *follow up* phone call in several days or during the first part of the next week. One of my prospects called me pleasantly persistent. I took that comment as a compliment. My goal is to be pleasantly persistent but not pushy. Calling someone day after day is taken as a pushy approach.

For some of my largest prospects, it took me weeks, if not months of *following up* to reach my contact. Continually scheduling *follow up* calls in my CRM system is part of being pleasantly persistent.

Prospects are generally busy, and meeting with a *sales professional* is not on the top of their list. That is because most *sales professionals* don't do a good job of selling the value of meeting with them. Your job is to have great *follow up*. Call several times, if necessary, to reach them and to convince them over the phone that it is important and of value to meet with you.

Next Steps and Follow Up

A major key to any *sales professional's* success is what I call *next steps*, always keeping *forward momentum*. In the martial arts, one of the main ways to gain maximum force when striking is to have *forward momentum* in tandem with your strike.

The same concept applies in the *mixed selling arts* world. Once you have identified a prospect, it should set off a series of *next steps*: How am I going to make my first contact to start gaining *intelligence* and begin to craft my *approach*? Will it be a site visit, or phone call inquiry? Internet research? This thinking sets off another series of *next steps*: schedule a *follow up* phone call; quick strategy session; then an appointment hopefully; and then another quick strategy session of *pre-call* plan and objectives. All of these considerations lead right into *next steps* after your first appointment in the **Closing Strategy stage**.

Saying you are going to *follow up* on a lead or prospect is not enough. What, exactly are you going to do? *Next steps* are the specifics of your *follow up*.

KEY TAKEAWAY

Next steps & follow up are major keys to anyone's success!

As when fishing, many *sales professionals* will get a nibble, pick up their gear and cast elsewhere.

BIG MISTAKE

Getting a nibble and immediately picking up your line and casting elsewhere!

ACTION!

"Action!" a Pride referee shouts out. PRIDE was the premier MMA competition in Japan (Purchased by the UFC in 2007). If both fighters are not pushing the action, the referee will shout out again, "Action!" If one or both of the fighters don't pick up the action, they will be given a *yellow card*. In PRIDE Fighting Championship events, a referee can give a *yellow card* for stalling. Not following the referee's commands can cost a competitor 10% of his winnings, money. Three *yellow cards* and the competitor was disqualified.

The same rules apply in the *MSA* world. For *sales professionals* to be or remain successful, occasionally they need to receive a *yellow card* from a sales manager or from themselves. ACTION! Studies have shown that all *sales professionals* experience bouts of "call reluctance". *Sales professionals* have to handle a lot of rejection; and at times in a *sales professional's* career, he or she will hesitate to make those next sales calls. This pausing is normal, but too much faltering will get the sales person multiple *yellow cards*.

Then there are times when *sales professionals* will stand around talking about how bad things are, talking about a perfect world in sales, filing some more of their paper work, doing another expense report or sales report, all which are "Non-revenue-generating sales activities". Too many of these time consumers will get you a *yellow card*. Actively pursuing *revenue-generating activities* is the only thing that will keep you from receiving a *yellow card*. It is the sales manager's and the company's ultimate responsibly to keep the sale force focused on *revenue-generating activities*. This is a HUGE requirement for both a *sales professional's* and company's success in sales. Not getting *yellow cards* and focusing the majority of a *sales professional's* time and *revenue-generating activities* are important concepts that will be *treading* through out every stage of the **SSC**.

KEY TAKEAWAY

The sales force MUST be focused on "revenue-generating activities" most of the time, in order to achieve success in sales.

Howard Behar, the former president of Starbucks, was quoted as saying, "A learning organization is useless unless it is a doing organization." The key, of course, is continually to learn as you are doing or to "Keep the *forward momentum* going".

Sales Professionals continually need to make more cold calls, *warm calls* and *follow up* calls. Any hot lead needs to be addressed immediately.

It is easy for *sales professionals* to stall, because prospecting involves lots of rejection. One just has to accept that fact. I have failed more than I have succeeded in sales, but I do know that I can create my own luck by what I call "stirring up the dust". After I make some prospecting calls and do *follow up* calls, I locate an opportunity. How is that? I went out and "Stirred up the dust". I created that opportunity; created my own luck.

KEY TAKEAWAY

"Strive for excellence, not perfection."

H. Jackson Brown, Jr.

The Pipeline

It is important to have a pipeline filled with multiple prospects at different stages of interest. The key to keeping a good pipeline filled and moving is constantly to be "stirring up the dust". Sales are activity driven. "Action!" should be heard from every *sales professional's* internal referee. It is time to "Stir up some more dust".

My analogy is that I always strive to be juggling several large opportunities at the same time. You are not going to win them all, so you better strive to be juggling more than one opportunity at a time. The best way to juggle a number of prospects effectively at a time is by using a good CRM (Customer Relationship Management) system.

Juggling Several Opportunities

The BIG MISTAKE I have seen made repeatedly is when a *sales professional*, frequently with his company's full backing, chases one huge opportunity, investing most if not all of the *sales professional's* time. If that opportunity does not materialize, the *sales professional's* pipeline is completely empty. *Sales professionals* have to always remember the saying "Don't put all your eggs in one basket".

At one of the companies I worked for, a fellow *sales professional* found a huge opportunity. He spent a majority of his time working on this very promising situation, to the detriment of his other prospecting activities. As I have seen occur many times in my sales career, the opportunity dragged on for months; and the customer ended up changing their mind, deciding that they could spend only one-quarter of the original projected amount. Ultimately, the project was never started.

> **BIG MISTAKE**
>
> **Sales Professionals putting all their eggs in one basket is a fast way to disaster.**

Such an end result is disastrous for the *sales professional*, especially if compensation is heavily commission based.

Speedy Response to Inquiries

If I get a "hot lead", I call them up immediately. If someone has just called in, I will make it a priority to call him or her right back, trying to avoid phone tag. I tell the prospect I had checked my messages just after he called. This is a subtlety, but it keeps me from appearing desperate. On numerous occasions, prospects have thanked me for my quick response and then gone on to tell me that I had called them back, explained our products and services, forwarded our information, and signed them up, all before my competitors even returned their calls. My competitors have received all three *yellow cards*, they have been disqualified and they lost the customer.

In many states, counties limit the number of fishing poles one person may use at one time. In many counties around the country I would not be allowed to bring 20 fishing poles and place them up and down a riverbank. In the sales world, that tactic is exactly what I am allowed to do and it is what I have to do to be successful. I have to be prospecting numerous opportunities at once and they can be managed very efficiently with a CRM system in place.

In a mixed martial arts competition, small things add up. A jab by itself may not win the fight, but jabs add up and ultimately can be key to a competitor's success in winning a fight. It's the same in sales. Prospecting activities over the days, weeks and months can and do add up.

Occasionally, I have thought how lucky I am to have been successful; but on closer observation, I have contacted lots of people and companies for that luck. Actively prospecting has kept me from getting a *yellow card* in sales.

This type of *revenue-generating activity* helps build a valuable sales pipeline.

Prospecting Never Stops

The strategies and techniques that I have described here are some of my favorites, which were developed over the years. My strategies and techniques are in constant refinement and improvement. A *sales professional's* prospecting never stops, whether with new prospective companies or with existing customers.

Companies, sales managers and *sales professionals* all need to remember to follow the MSA methodology and never to stop learning and improving.

Once you have accomplished your first goal of securing an appointment, what is next? You try to close the deal in the **Closing stage**.

KEY TAKEAWAY

"Don't judge each day by the harvest you reap but by the seeds that you plant."

Robert Louis Stephenson, writer

6

Closing Strategy Stage

There are many Truths and Universal Truths

Selling is an Art and a Process

Why do customers buy?

Lower the Risk to Buy

Can You Afford to Close This Deal?

"Closing the deal" is the most important part of sales. If the company and its sales force do not close many or any deals, neither will last very long. There have been mountains of books written on the subject. My experience and research is on closing B2B sales both with *projects* and *programs*. Countless closing strategies and techniques have been in use for years, but they need to be updated and refined. Many of the techniques are still basically the same. It is the *environment* that has forced changes in being able to *increase your odds* of closing business in today's ultra-competitive environment. Many large studies have found that it now takes more time to close sales than in previous years. This situation reinforces the need for companies to be more strategic in their approaches to selling.

It is the *set up*, the way you build up to execute a particular move, which is the most important. For example, an MMA competitor has a great leg kick attack or arm bar that could help to win the fight, but it is how he maneuvers his opponent at the right time and place to apply it that decides whether he succeeds. I consider myself to be a good finisher in grappling competition; but, as always, my biggest challenge is figuring out how I am going to *set up* the finishing move. Similarly in the *MSA* world, you cannot just ask for the order (close the deal) before you have created the proper *set up* to go for a close.

Mario Sperry is one of my favorite MMA and Brazilian Jiu-Jitsu expert instructors. In his DVD training series, he mentions that one of his favorite sweeps, a move to reverse your position, has been in use since he was a teenager. The basic move is very similar, but the *set up* has changed over the years. The basic sweep is a *Universal Truth*, an idea or move that works under pressure for a large percentage of the people who learn it. The move succeeds in training and most importantly, it works in competition under pressure.

The late, great John H. Patterson of NCR - Nation Cash Register, came up with his own system, a step-by-step process that focused on the customer's problems and not just features of his product. His thinking and process has become legendary and is still studied by many in sales today. Mr. Patterson's thinking was somewhat the start of a solution selling approach, and by following a process, one is aided to "Increasing the Odds" of success. His routines of focusing on the customer and utilizing a process in sales have been found to be *Universal Truths*.

KEY TAKEAWAY

Sales is a process, not an event! The same goes for any stage of selling.

Just because your company theorizes that a sales strategy or technique has a high percentage of success, do not accept it until it has been proven several times to work for others in your company. Following the MSA methodology, I have learned not only from my own experiences to improve my strategies and techniques but also from the successes and failures of fellow *sales professionals*, sales managers, sales consultants and authors. As a result, I am proving that my strategies work every day in the trenches, NOT just in theory. Whenever there is interaction between a B2B *sales professional* and a prospect/ customer, it is an "art" not a science. However, there is a but. As you continually try to make many aspects of sales a science rather than an art, creating processes, systems and models helps to increase the odds of success by reducing the art.

If I seem to be repeating myself, this is intentional. There are many ideas, strategies and techniques that are *threaded*, code word for repeated, throughout every stage of the **Strategic Selling Cycle** and this book. I follow Senior Grandmaster Ed Parker's saying, "Slow to learn, slow to forget". It takes me a while to get something down; but once I learn it, I am good at remembering it and applying it under pressure. That is one of my goals for anyone who reads this book, not only learn new ideas but be able to apply them in realistic situations.

Companies and *sales professionals* should become processes dependent and not people dependent. The **Strategic Selling Cycle** is a group of processes for how sales orders flow through a company. Each stage of the **SSC** needs to be turned into a process and using proven processes over and over again will definitely *increase your odds* of success. In addition, any parts of the **SSC** that can be systemized and automated will enhance continued improvement.

> **KEY TAKEAWAY**
> **Companies and Sales Professionals need to become process dependent, not people dependent.**

There are many examples why these sayings are powerful. One example could be that one should not rely on a sales manager for the *next steps* in many sales situations. There should be a process, comprised of best practices, which help guide *sales professionals* through a sale. Yes, the sales manager is and should be a great additional resource to coach and assist when needed; but the sales force needs to be able to rely on proven processes, because the sales manager cannot be available to assist every time. Being dependent on a process, not a person, is especially important when today's sales managers are seeing an increase in the numbers of *sales professionals* reporting to them.

The **Strategic Selling Cycle** is part of a methodology that helps companies continually improve and learn by following proven processes. One of the best examples of becoming process dependent is the utilization of a CRM system. All *sales professionals* should remember that this saying applies to them: "Do not become totally dependent on yourself". Instead, become dependent on the processes and then you will continually manage the processes of your sales efforts.

Sometimes, you will achieve a quick close, but remember that the *follow up* after the close is still a continuation of a process. Most B2B, business-to-business sales situations, today are comprised of many steps that follow a process. Utilizing a CRM system will help sales forces automate these *next steps*. Following a process will help the sales force keep on track.

For example, a potential customer tells you that he wants to meet with you to "get going" with your company but to call him back in two weeks. This should start a *follow up* process. Send a thank you card or email saying you are looking forward to working with him and *schedule* the phone call. Remember the important point in the **Prospecting Strategy stage**: You must volunteer to call him back in two weeks to "Keep the Ball in Your Court!" These actions then can be scheduled in your CRM system.

Studies have shown that it takes multiple touches with a prospect to close a sale. By "Keeping the ball in your court", you have another chance to continue the discussion, strengthen your relationship, and build your case. *Follow up* is the only way you will be able to continue the steps to the close. Far too many *sales professionals* have poor *follow up* or give up after the first or second contact with the prospect and that is a BIG MISTAKE.

> **BIG MISTAKE**
>
> **Not following up with prospects guarantees that you will be a statistic on the next sales study as one of the low performers.**

As I have mentioned, the ranges cross in the MMA competition. An example could be punching and kicking. The **Strategic Selling Cycle** does the same. You continually qualify the prospect to see if they are a fit for your company's products and services. Also, you are always prospecting with existing customers: the **Expanding stage**.

One important note is to make sure you adapt your selling process to fit your prospect's buying processes. Companies' sales processes that are not flexible and adaptable to the environment will not be very successful.

> **KEY TAKEAWAY**
> **Adapt your selling process to the prospect's buying process.**

Sales Tools and Sales Knowledge

Access and availability of sales resources is a large challenge for many companies across the USA and around the world. A company's resources to assist the sales force in closing of business should be easily accessible to the sales team members. I have found that in many small and large companies these resources are not very easy to access.

While working for an international company, I went to sales training for the new sales force. It was called "First 90 Days", because it was for the newly reorganized sales force after being in the field for the first 90 days. During the training event, and it was an "event", they said that anything we might need was on a website. All a *sales professional* had to do was go to the website and get it. Wow! What a BIG MISTAKE! What the top sales managers and executives did not understand was the difference between available and easily accessible. After the training event, I went back to the office and tried to check out the website mentioned in the training. It was difficult to get into, very difficult to navigate and the test downloads did not print out correctly. I never could get anyone to help me figure out how to access any of the supposed great resources.

This company's thinking is like telling one of my new students that I have over 100 martial arts training DVDs that can help them out without telling them where I live. Even if they did come over, they would not know which one they should begin with. This is a classic mistake, and many of the recent studies that I have read confirm this problem. Many companies have no centralized up-to-date knowledge center that is easily accessible to their sales force.

> **BIG MISTAKE**
>
> **Many companies forget that sales knowledge and sales tools might be "available", but that is not the same as "easily accessible".**

Once a company makes its sales resources easily accessible, it should teach the sales force how to utilize those tools. In the mixed martial arts world, I could point a student to a chest full of training equipment. Easily accessible right? Not without proper training on the equipment's function and value for the fighter.

Companies and sales managers need to teach their sales force how to use the tools provided. More isn't always better, especially if no one knows how to utilize them most effectively.

Simple vs. Complex sales

Sales professionals also need to know if they are going to be involved in a simple or complex sales cycle. Simple sales are exactly what the name implies, fairly straight forward sales processes. Complex sales might involve several decision makers and multiple group presentations. Typically, complex sales are for larger dollar amounts and have a much longer timeline to the close. Not all sales people are suited for both simple and complex sales. The company and the *sales professional* need to know what the type of sale will be in order to plan the steps for a successful close. For a complex sale, identifying the entire buying group is crucial to *increasing your odds* for closing. A sales team approach is usually the best tactic to use for a complex sale. The bottom line is to be *aware* of the differences before starting the selling process.

Why Customers Buy

There is no single answer to the question of "Why do customers buy?" This is a very talked about topic and this is why sales is an art and not a perfect science. There are some *Truths* and *Universal Truths,* but "No one is the holder of the truth", to again quote the late great martial artist Bruce Lee. Many sales experts whose articles I have read sound like they are the holders of *The Truth,* they know the single reason all customers buy. They might have discovered one *Truth* or even a *Universal Truth,* but there are many reasons customers will buy. Sometimes the reasons change as the environment changes.

Remember that even *Universal Truths* are like best practices. They are not a guarantee of success. They just have a proven track record and will *increase your odds* if followed.

My experiences show that there are some *Truths* and *Universal Truths* to the question of "Why do customers buy?" One way I have found out why customers buy was simply to ask them. Asking both new and existing customers why they buy from my company and me has brought up some very interesting lessons. Here are some:

> *-People buy from people they like.*
> *-Customers' perception of value "is" reality.*
> *-Make it easy to buy.*
> *-Lower the risk to buy.*
> *-Make it a risk not to take action.*

People buy from people they like

A goal of all *sales professionals* should be to build a good relationship with their customers to protect them against losing the business to a competitor. A big reason why the customer will buy is if he/she has a good relationship with the *sales professional* or somebody else who works for the company. Many times, the customer will be buying an inferior product or service from someone they have a relationship with or are friends with outside of business hours. Due to a personal relationship, such a competitor is a tough prospect to change. I have a good friend who is a very successful *sales professional* and is great at building both friendships and relationships with his customers. He told me he feels that it helps solidify the relationship if the customer thinks you care about their success. I agree.

Outside activities such as those mentioned earlier in the **Prospecting Strategy stage**, i.e., sporting events, dinners and shows, are also huge building blocks to developing stronger relationships within a company.

I always try to strengthen the relationship between my company and an existing customer by including others in my company who seem to bond with the key decision makers. I have many great customers who like me but have stronger relationships with others in my company. That is one of the "secrets" to my success. I *leverage* my relationships as well as other co-workers' relationships.

> **KEY TAKEAWAY**
>
> **The strongest bonds with customers exist when there are relationships with you and others in your company.**

Customers' Perception of Value is Reality

I have had to abandon an opportunity because what I thought or knew wasn't going to change what the prospect thought.

This idea has been around forever but is repeated frequently now by many sales experts: You might know in your heart that your product or service is ten times better than your competitor's, but if the customer "thinks" their current vendor provides a better total package, then that is reality for the customer.

This can become very frustrating when you, the supposed expert knows better, but the customer still believes that they are using the best solution or vendor. In their mind, that is reality.

It is up to the *sales professional* to provide the right type of backup information to help change the prospect's thinking. One of the main jobs of any *sales professional* is to build value and a case for why it is in the best interests of the prospect to utilize your company's services.

Make it Easy to Buy and Easy to do Business With

This is a concept that I used unconsciously for years. Then I started to use it consciously as a strategy once I realized the power of this idea. This idea should be turned into a strategy for every company. Think about why you buy from someone. If they make it difficult and a lot of trouble to spend your money, then you might choose someone else. If a company continually bills you incorrectly and you have to call them to get it straightened out, you will probably be looking for another vendor.

As a sales person, nothing can make my job more challenging than if it is difficult for the customer to do business with my company. I have a saying: "The toughest part of my job isn't closing new business but relying on my company to provide what we have promised." I will cover this saying in more detail in **Fulfillment & Support Strategy stages**.

Following are examples of how I have tried to make it easy for the customer to buy from me. These are some situations and techniques that have helped me be successful at closing more sales. The possibilities are endless, but companies and sales forces need to look constantly for new ways to make it easy for their prospects and customers to buy and continue to buy from them.

Example #1: When I worked for Warner Lambert, many of our promotions were available for purchase through my customers' monthly order guides. Many of the items for each department were optional to bring into the stores, and it was up to the department managers to decide which optional items would sell best in their stores. Our sales team would come in with promotional flyers, which listed their company's order numbers and details. I would fill out the flyer for the department manager, have him sign it and then I would turn it in to the sales manager in our company who handled the ordering for that particular chain's headquarters. If it was a large promotion that the customer agreed to purchase, I would offer to help set up the displays, make shelf space or whatever would "Make it easy for them to buy" the promotion. On the other hand, if I would have trusted that the customer would remember to order my promotion in his company's buying guide, the customer might have realized that our promotion would create more work by his having to set up promotional material and find room to display it. Then, he might have thought it was too much trouble and never have ordered our promotional products. I sold numerous promotions into stores using this strategy.

Example #2: When I worked at Simplex, I used the lesson of "Make it easy for them to buy" successfully in several different ways. I was in Service Sales when I first started working for Simplex, and I sold testing and maintenance agreements for the systems we sold. I also sold maintenance agreements for our competitors' equipment. Fire alarm systems were the largest category of equipment Simplex sold.

I would go out to prospects and try to convince them it was in their best interest to have our trained experts test and maintain their fire alarm systems. I used the technique *Good, Better, Best* to sell the agreements. We could customize our testing and maintenance agreement in numerous ways. There could be so many choices that it became confusing to the customer on which option to consider or buy. My technique was to present them with three options; from least expensive to the most costly. They were the testing only option, testing plus panel coverage or testing plus full coverage on the panel plus all other devices, e.g., smoke detectors, heat detectors, etc.

Most customers were not doing testing or maintenance, so any option was going to be a new budget expense. Many times the customer would ask me which option I would recommend. I would suggest the middle or "better" option, testing and panel only. Then I would explain that they would be in compliance with the state's testing regulations and be able to budget for any unexpected large cost of panel failure. Most of the agreements bought were the "Better" option. Sometimes, I was surprised and the customer would choose the "best" option. This meant a larger sale for me.

This technique worked well for me. I was the only *sales professional* for service in Boise and lead our office to be number one in the nation for Service Sales both years I was in that division.

Example #3: Another sales position I held at Simplex was as a building system sales representative. I sold commercial equipment: fire alarms, phone, intercom and security systems. I would use a technique known as *bundling*. Today many companies use this technique as part of a strategic advantage over companies that do not offer multiple products or services. Our local phone company, Qwest, offers *bundle* packages that include landline phone, cellular phone and Internet services all packaged together. They can offer a lower price than if you bought each service separately. Now, it is becoming common for companies to offer their products and services together in a *bundled* offer.

I did the same thing on many of the offering opportunities at Simplex. A bidding situation is the best example of the strength of *bundling*. I might have been bidding on a new building that needed all of the systems we offered. I would bid one *bundled* price for the whole *project*. This would stop the buyers from shopping each system I offered. One of my systems might not have the lowest price, but my *bundled* price for all systems needed could be the lowest. Even if my *bundled* price was the same as two or three vendors' combined bids for systems needed for the project, usually the buyer would go with me because they would only have to deal with one vendor instead of multiple vendors. I would also guarantee that all my systems would smoothly integrate together. The prospect would only have to deal with one company invoicing them and one place to go for questions, help or service. I made it easy for them to buy from me and easy for them to do business with me.

Even though this is a B2C – business-to-consumer example, McDonalds is one of the greatest at the *bundling* technique. "I will take a number 3", which includes, by the way, a burger, fries and a drink. Wow, did they steal my idea? Of course not, they just are using a *Universal Truth*, which says that it's easy to buy and buy more, with the technique of *bundling*.

Example #4: When I worked at Kinko's, many times I would make up what I called "Kinko's at a Glance" sheets for my customers. These were one page Kinko's letterheads with a brief overview of our two local branches, top products we offered, contact information, addresses, phone numbers, emails addresses and contact names. Then I would include customer specific information, such as discounts.

Usually, the customers posted it up on the wall for quick reference. Many times, when they needed to use our services, it was a rush. The "Kinko's at a Glance" sheet was a nice tool for them to refer to with all pertinent information to make an order.

A national account manager for Kinko's was in town and talking to me about his problem of getting consistent pricing and overall information out to all the locations of a large national company based out of Boise, Idaho. I mentioned how successful my "Kinko's at a Glance" was working for me, and the national account manager asked me to help him work up one for his account. This was a simple but powerful selling strategy. Today, I would combine a hard copy and an online ABC COMPANY at a Glance, containing easy contact information for any questions or new orders.

In today's ultra-competitive marketplace, it should be the goal of all companies to make it easy for the customer to buy. If your company doesn't, a competitor will.

Lower the Risk to Buy

Recent studies show that the sales cycles are getting longer. One of the biggest reasons decision makers stall or make no decision is because the *sales professional* did not *"lower the risk"* or make is easy to take action. In today's fast-paced business environment, buyers are more skeptical and are under more pressure than ever before. Making a mistake by choosing the wrong product or service can cost them money, time and in extreme cases, even their jobs.

As I mentioned in several of the **SSC** stages, you should try constantly to reduce the risk of purchasing from you and your company. Testimonials help back up that what you and your company say is actually true. This is especially important for a new prospect.

Providing references, supplying letters of recommendation and, reinforcing a successful track record of helping others by solving the companies' problems all aid in lowering the risk of change. Furthermore,

103

if your company has a recognizable name and a long track record, these credentials will help to reduce the risk, as well.

A simple B2C – business-to-consumer example is my personal experience with Costco, the price club and mass discounter. I choose to buy many of my personal purchases from Costco, because there is very low risk to me. Generally, I have found that they sell quality products and offer an outstanding return policy. I have no reservation about buying items from Costco, because I know that if I am unhappy in any way they will take my purchased product back with a smile. If I do return something, most of the time I end up spending more in the store than the item I returned.

> **KEY TAKEAWAY**
>
> **A goal to closing a sale is to "lower the risk" of meeting with you, buying from you and believing in you. The only risk should be if they don't choose you.**

Make it a Risk <u>Not</u> to Take Action

It is crucial to demonstrate to prospects and customers that it is a risk not to utilize your company's products and services and to build a case, with evidence, that **no action** could cost them problems in the near future. As mentioned before, the book, "Solution Selling: Creating Buyers in Difficult Selling Markets" by Michael T. Bosworth, is a very useful sales tool. Bosworth explains the need to build a case that a problem requires immediate attention or it can cost the customer considerable time and money. Even though his book was written years ago, it is still relevant in today's business environment.

You have to build a case, with evidence, e.g., with customer recommendations that state how much time and money your company has saved them. Most, if not all, prospects and customers currently have huge "to do" lists, and it is in the *sales professional's* interest to make the problem perceived as big enough to be placed at the top of the customer's "to do" list.

Remember, by making the problem important enough to take action, you will ensure that your customer does not get a *yellow card* for stalling. Keep in mind that in the mixed martial arts competitions in Japan, the awarding of a *yellow card* for stalling can cost a competitor money or even the match.

Know your Competition

In the MMA competition, top competitors will watch and study films of their opponents. What are his strengths and weaknesses? How can his weakness be exploited? Similarly, in *mixed selling arts* competition, it is crucial that you and your company know the competitions' strengths and weaknesses.

Studies have shown that many companies are still challenged to get competitive information to their sales force on a timely basis. Companies need to remember the difference between "available" and easily "accessible". Make sure competitive information is valuable and easily accessible to the sales force.

At Kinko's, the sales force was required to do mystery shops of our competitors. To me, having high paid *sales professionals* doing price checks was a BIG MISTAKE. Many times, the businesses we were checking on were not our primary competitors. Kinko's was on the right path in trying to gain competitive information, but management utilized one of the most expensive ways to obtain the information.

Companies and sales forces need to make sure they know who their competitors are and to build *intelligence* on them, which can be shared with the entire sales force.

Personally, I have always kept track of my competitors. After submitting bids, I would try to find out what the competitors' bids were. Then I would document the details of what each bid included. At my present position, I know my competitors very well and I have very detailed information about them. Although my customers have offered much of this information to me without even being asked, I still ask a few questions, such as "How much did your previous agency charge?", "What did you like and dislike about your previous agency?", "Why did you decide to go with us?" and "What was the deciding factor?" These types of questions need to be asked and are invaluable for strategizing against your competitors. Patterns will emerge. Each company and each *sales professional* of a particular company has strengths and weaknesses. It will be your job to minimize their strengths and exploit their weaknesses, just as in an MMA competition.

As mentioned in the **Prospecting Strategy stage**, I try to find out if a customer has been using another vendor before considering tactics for the **Closing Strategy stage**. Once I know the prospect's suppliers, I am able to craft my strategy to focus on my company's strengthens and the competitors' weaknesses.

> **KEY TAKEAWAY**
> **It is always best to know your competitor's strengths and weaknesses before you step in the cage!**

Stories Sell and Features Tell

Understanding and incorporating the idea of "Stories sell and features tell" into your sales skills is one of the most powerful tools I have developed during my sales career. One of my prior sales managers wrote me a letter of recommendation that pointed out what he had observed on several sales calls.

> *"Scott built a model for reaching decision-makers with a focus on education that was adopted by our entire sales team. After this initial education step, Scott would engage the customer in a strategic plan to help their business through his solutions. These methods closed many projects; but more importantly, Scott developed relationships with recurring revenue streams."*

He was referring to my method of using stories to sell, educate and build value; not the traditional probing techniques with features and benefits. A common recommendation from many sales books and sales experts is that on a first sales call you should do little talking and use probing questions to get the customer to tell you about their problems and needs. I agree and have used these techniques, but I have found that customers "keep their cards close to their chests". You have to earn their trust. Many times, it appears to the prospect that the questioning simply is a way to manipulate them to your close. Generally, they aren't going to tell you every pressing problem their company has. You have to build trust and credibility before they start to open up.

Sometimes, prospects do not really know they have a problem that you can solve. A little *intelligence* from your pre-call detective work in the **Prospecting stage** will help you decide which stories to tell. Stories help to let the prospect know what you and your company do and how you have helped other similar companies solve their problems/needs. Stories help distinguish you and your company by letting the prospect know that you are not only familiar with their KBI's (Key Business

Issues) but have successfully helped others solve theirs. You and your company want to differentiate yourselves from the competition but, more importantly, to show how those differences are going to help your customers solve their problems.

This storytelling technique can be used by giving the prospect a quick overview about your company's products and services. (Bulletin to all *sales professionals*: most of your prospects <u>do not</u> care about your company's history but rather how your company can help them be more competitive, so keep your company history brief!) Then I proceed to tell them stories about how my company and I have helped other companies similar to theirs solve problems. This is where the *intelligence* from the **Prospecting stage** pays off. If I know they have some particular challenges or problems, I choose a story of a company that had similar challenges and problems that we solved. Better yet, I have a success story from one of the customer's letters of recommendation that I dropped off to the current prospect in the **Prospecting stage**.

Also, craft your stories to accentuate your company's strengths; and, if you find out they use a particular competitor, craft your stories to highlight any weaknesses the competitor might have where your company shines. Never talk badly about the competition! Tell your company's strengths, which might bring to light some of the competitor's weaknesses, without your naming them.

Remember to always think from the customer's point of view. You said you have the best copy machines, network hardware, phone systems, etc. Always try to answer the most common questions in the back of your prospect's mind, "So what? What will your offering do for my company to reduce costs, to be more competitive, increase revenues, etc?" Until you start to answer the basic questions, your customer really does not care or believe whatever you offer will do anything more than cost him more money than it should.

The technique of telling short, carefully crafted stories is especially helpful for a customer who won't open up. There have been numerous times when I was relating a story of how we helped another company when the prospect stopped me and said, "Boy, we have that problem too!" or "The XYZ department has that problem ever year." Now that you have gotten them talking, it is the time to probe to get them talking about their challenges and problems.

It is most effective to make all your company's solutions and stories specific to companies that are similar or that the customer might recognize.

One of the toughest parts of sales is to uncover a need for your products or services. The customers may not know they have a problem or a need. It is the *sales professional's* job to uncover a problem or need. Stories help the customers visualize problems and solutions. Stories also force the *sales professional* to be more solution oriented and consultative in their sales calls, instead of focusing solely on trying to sell the customer on their products and services.

Studies have shown a major shift of companies trying to train sales forces to be more solution focused. Training sales forces to use success stories as a part of their sales process will help sales forces be more focused on solutions.

I once was told by top sales management of Simplex that I should sell the reason a company should test and maintain its fire alarms, "Because it is the right thing to do." On the contrary, I found that by stressing that the *pain*, problems associated by not properly maintaining the prospect's fire alarm; could result in unhappy employees, tenants, customers and the liability, I got a lot of prospects to act. I have found that people will avoid *pain* more than they will react to the status quo or because "It is the right thing to do."

Stories have helped me to uncover problems and issues that were unknown to the customer. Most industries have many of the same challenges that they are facing. Telling stories first helps you get to what really interests your prospect. Prospects do not have all day, so by letting them know up front that you are familiar with their challenges will build trust. Why should they have to teach you their industry? Remember, you are supposed to be the expert.

Stories of how you helped other companies with similar challenges are great probing techniques. Success stories are a way of probing without having to seem to be manipulating by asking a line of questions.

When I worked for Simplex in the Time and Attendance division, I would tell stories of how we had helped other companies automate their payroll systems. I would present backup documentation of a large payroll association study that found if a company changed from a manual to an automated system, they could expect to save two percent of their annual payroll. I had one customer with a payroll that was several million dollars per year and their ROI - return on investment was recouped in less than one year. Plus, they achieved the savings of the "hassle factor", making their job substantially easier. This was just as important to the people I was talking to as the money savings. I did not pull out a bunch of fancy brochures for every sales call, but instead, I pulled out stories that solved customers' problems with our solutions.

> **KEY TAKEAWAY**
> **Stories sell and features tell.**
> **Better yet, success stories sell and features tell.**

Here is a word of advice when using findings from credible studies to help reinforce the reason a customer should buy from you: It is always best to use such studies in combination with your prospect's own numbers. I did not just throw out the percentage; instead, I took the most important next step. I tied them to the prospective company's own numbers so they could truly see the impact on their company. Thus, the findings are personal.

Frequently deals or opportunities are lost because of the customer getting numerous *yellow cards* due to indecision. This hesitancy can result when the *sales professional* has uncovered a problem but did not take the time to educate the customer on the significance of the problem or its potential to get worse. The *sales professional* needs to take as much time as necessary asking the customer to put dollar figures to their problem. Combining their own numbers with studies can help focus the size and cost of the problem or problems that have been uncovered.

While working at Kinko's, I would secure appointments by using my *"Just want to give you a quick update"* technique. I would then tell them I would highlight the last two year's changes at Kinko's in ten minutes. This is the same thing I had told them on the phone to "sell" the appointment. I would tell stories of how different products and services helped solve problems with companies similar to theirs, and I would go through a coupon book that I was going to give them. This was a very effective technique to get the prospects talking. Some prospects would tell me, "We have a big job like that coming up in two months and it always shuts this department down to complete it". Plus, the discount coupons *lowered the risk* for buying to try our services. I would also offer a sample of any product they were interested in.

The above discussion is an example of what Mario Sperry, MMA and Brazilian Jiu-Jitsu expert, stresses. "All the moves and techniques I show you are connected". This is a very important point that applies to sales success. In the previous example, I combined "Just wanted to give you a quick update", "Stories Sell" and giving coupons to *lower the risk* to buy. Remember that many strategies and techniques can be *combined* to be even more effective.

Using success stories, not titles such as Solutions Expert, helps companies and their sales forces to be more focused on solution selling. A major study found that there is a universal trend of companies focusing on solution selling. It has reached the point now that most companies have taken it to the extreme. They are naming companies ABC Solutions and *sales professionals* are given titles of Solutions Sales Consultants. However, prospective buyers are starting to tune out the "Solutions" title that many companies are professing. This is similar to businesses stating that "Their prices CAN NOT be beat!" After a while, customers tune these gimmicks out.

> **KEY TAKEAWAY**
> **Make all your company's solutions into success stories!**

Value Propositions

There is a lot of discussion concerning companies' value propositions. One of the companies I worked for used the term in their presentations, "Our Company's value proposition is...". Studies have shown that many executives blame their company's poor sales performance on the fact they have a weak value proposition. A value proposition should contain short and concise statements of what your company provides that is/are different and superior to a competitors' offer, or what the customer will achieve by attempting to do it themselves. What is the unique benefit or payoff to using your company's services?

Remember, everything is *connected*. Having great stories regarding how your company has helped its customers overcome major challenges builds great value propositions. What does your company do for your customers? What do you do differently or uniquely compared to your competitors? Make a list of compelling success stories and then utilize them to help build a great value proposition for your company. Value propositions and stories tailored to the prospects challenges and problems can be very persuasive.

Some *sales professionals* make the mistake of saying things like,

"I am a sales representative for ABC Company, which has been in business for over 50 years...."

I am in sales, I work for XYZ company and we sell the best copy machines in the USA and...."

Value means different things to different people. Make sure your value proposition is not canned. It has to be modified once, through *intelligence,* specific problems are uncovered with a particular prospect or customer.

Intangibles vs. Tangibles

When I was going through the interview process with Simplex, a big part of the interview concerned how I felt about selling an intangible, a service vs. a product. If only I had known then that all *sales professionals* should become experts at selling intangibles, service and knowledge, not just products. Products become commodities very fast in today's competitive world.

I was attending a business luncheon where the speaker was Mike Adkins, former CEO of a local computer manufacturer. He made a comment that illustrated my point exactly. He said that in this day and age computers are commodities, "until they are deployed." What a great point! Not many people care what brand a computer is, just that it works and helps them in their day-to-day job. At a higher level in a company, how does the computer vendor support the equipment after the sale? Do they offer services to teach the customer how to utilize the equipment most effectively to stay competitive? The successful computer vendor must offer more than just a bunch of boxes that sit on the employees' desks.

When I worked for Intermountain Technology Group, I talked to customers about their problems and how our company's services could help their company run smoother and more profitably. The equipment and software were part of our solution to solve their problems. I used the same approach when I was selling for Simplex's Time and Attendance division. I never once brought in any of our equipment. The customers never saw the equipment until it showed up at time of installation. The equipment was a piece of my solution, not the solution. Many of the other *sales professionals* would do demos on their laptops and were rarely successful at closing new business. They were selling a product, a time clock, not a solution for a company's time and attendance

111

challenges.

The computer industry is an excellent example of an industry in which many of their products have turned into commodities. In 1993, Louis V. Gerstner, Jr. became IBM chairman and CEO. The company had been experiencing billion dollar losses, and Gerstner went to customers to try to figure out what was wrong. The main thing he discovered was that IBM had become a company that sold products, not a company that helped their customers with their problems. He found out years ago what many companies still have not figured out today; you need to turn all your products into services.

A number of my sales have been achieved because the customer bought a solution to a need. They were also buying me. I was representing my company's interest in their needs and had relentlessly pursued or wooed them by letting them know that I cared about their problems. Showing that you care builds relationships, loyalty and sales. Interest and caring are intangibles.

KEY TAKEAWAY

Let your products be a piece of the solution, not THE solution.

Sales forces need to focus on how their products and services will help customers. Using stories which "verb it", to quote Professor Skip Hancock, will help stop *sales professionals* from talking about products, which are nouns. This is a vital strategy to help stop companies' products from becoming commodities.

KEY TAKEAWAY

Turn every product into a service and every service into solutions.

Probing

Stories are a great way to start the probing process. When the prospect/customer starts talking, that is the time where the saying, "You have two ears and one mouth; listen twice as much as you talk," is so important to a *sales professional.*

When using old school probing techniques, one has to be careful not to come off canned or manipulative. That is why I recommend starting with stories. I even use stories to help clarify a point. If you have uncovered a problem, try to tell a quick story to see if you are on the right track. "We helped ABC Corp. reduce their outstanding account receivables by... is that similar to your problem?" Many in sales recommend repeating what the customer has said to help you ensure you are on the same page, but you have to be careful. The *sales professional* can sound like a parrot, scripted and insincere.

For good questioning, the *sales professional* has to know their company's products and services, the strengths and weaknesses of the competition and challenges typically faced by customers. Many would disagree with me by saying that every customer and situation is different. In the MMA competitions every competitor is different, but there are many similarities between them. Do they favor grappling or striking? Many of the grappling and striking moves have become similar over time.

When probing in sales, it is difficult to uncover and further explore a problem if you have no experience from a similar situation with another customer. If you discover a problem which is new to you and/or your company, you might have to come back for another meeting armed with help from others to further explore the opportunity. If you find a good solution to a new problem, then you and your company are armed with expertise and knowledge that possibly can be used for other new prospects or even your existing customers in the **Expanding Stage**.

When a prospective customer finally calls you for the meeting that you have been pursuing for quite some time, it is a perfect time to probe for their problems and issues. The first thing you want to ask is "What has changed?" Many times in the past, the prospect may have felt that they did not have an immediate need for your products and services. However, now they have contacted you for a meeting, so most likely something has changed. There is no better time to probe for their real problems than when they ask you for a meeting. It usually means that they have a pressing need and will be much more likely to discuss all their problems and challenges openly.

You are trying to create the sense of urgency that the customer's problem needs to be addressed and is big enough or will become big enough that planning needs to be started now. "Action!" With your customer references and stories, you will have *lowered the risk* to take action. Again, the trick is to make it a big risk <u>not</u> to take action now but little to no risk by taking action with you and your company.

113

Talk Offs / Talk Tracks

Companies need to arm their sales force with a good list of *talk offs* for probing and closing. I have heard them called both *talk offs* and *talk tracks* but I use the term *talk offs*. *Talk offs* are another example of my saying, "It's not what you say but how you say it". A customer may stop you in the middle of a sales call and ask, "What do you charge for your services?" This is a very predicable question, and it shouldn't be a big surprise to any *sales professional*. A company should arm their sales force with some good responses to help the *sales professional* to make adaptations to the response to fit their style. An example that I would be comfortable using to respond to the question is, "It depends. We really do a lot of different things for different companies. We can work together to see how we can help your company and then I will work up some costs for you." I have had a customer press me for costs and I will give them a range for similar type situations. Just as in the mixed martial arts, you better not be surprised if your opponent tries to take you down.

Talk offs are similar to the martial arts pre-set techniques. For example, if an opponent throws a right cross, then you will do A-B-C to defend. Many people in martial arts criticize pre-set, prearranged moves and many times, I do too! The difference is that, realistic, simple, high percentage pre-planned moves do work. Opponents often throw somewhat predictable attacks. Practicing realistic, simple, *high percentage moves* helps a student become "more confident and, most importantly, competent", to quote Professor Skip Hancock.

Pre-planned lines of questions, stories and responses help prepare a *sales professional* when talking to prospects and do increase the odds of closing more sales.

It is very important in sales to gain credibility. Letters of recommendation provided in the **Prospecting Stage** will help start to build credibility. Then, success stories will aid in building more credibility. Be careful <u>not</u> to ask probing questions that are obvious. "Would you like to make the company more money?" or "How would you like to save eight hours a week of your time?" These kinds of questions can raise a red flag to the buyer that you are either inexperienced, insincere or both. Insincerity can be a credibility killer.

Be sure to have a good line of intelligent questions. Having too many general questions is not useful. "How's business going?" That is a question I would save for an existing customer. Try not to sound like every other *sales professional* that they meet. Stories help start a conversation and can lead to more specific questions. They can also make you sound unique and experienced. If your *sales professionals* aren't armed with some intelligent questions for *talk offs*, then they are more apt to miss opportunities. Crafting questions around your company's strengths and your competitors' weaknesses will lead to better questions and help to uncover problems.

Having good *talk offs* and preset questions to further explore a problem are highly recommended as training aids for the sales force.

In the MMA world, there are probing techniques that must be taught before any competitor's first competition and continually used in training there after. Throwing low leg kicks forces the opponent to drop his hands to defend. This is a very common situation that happens at all levels, but especially in the beginning levels. Any good instructor has drills that teach new students to throw some low kicks to see if an opponent drops his hands.

The reason many in both the MMA and the *MSA* do not like preset techniques/questions, is that the ones they have used before were not realistic. In the sales world, studies have shown a major trend for all sales forces to be trained in "solution selling". Good, non-manipulative questions are a must. *Sales professionals* need to act like a doctor who is trying to diagnose; they should not try to interrogate and manipulate.

There are many books that cover open and close ended questioning. Just make sure the questions are continually being "refined" so that they are useful at uncovering and understanding the true problems of your customers. With probing, this rule is never truer:
"It isn't what you say but how you say it"!

What didn't you like about my proposal?
vs.
How will our services help you and your company?

Do you think your department does well overall?
vs.
Do you think your department is higher or lower than the twenty-percent national average?

Is everything going pretty well with your current vendor?
vs.
Tell me more about the problems with the missed shipments.

Do you have any needs now?

vs.

What is your biggest challenge with your account receivables this year?

One person that I consider at the black belt level at *talk offs* is Art Sobczak, president of Business By Phone Inc. I recommend checking out his Ezine, newsletter, at www.businessbyphone. com.

Project vs. Program

I have mentioned the concepts of *projects* and *programs* several times so far. *Programs* are orders that repeat. A *project* is a one-time sale; it could be a $10 or a $1,000,000 sale. If there were additional service after the sale, the on-going service part would be a *program*.

Understanding the difference is one of the most important ideas for any company and *sales professional* to understand. Knowing and understanding the difference can guarantee more sales. Remember to *thread* proven ideas throughout every stage of the **Strategic Selling Cycle**.

The idea is pretty easy, but just as with many things in business or sales, knowing is easy and doing is the hard part. If there is an opportunity for a customer continually to buy the same product or service, the hardest part is usually getting the first order to prove yourself.

The costs for reorders are substantially lower both in terms of time and money. Many companies have finally realized that it costs a substantial amount to bid every item or service they need every time. Many enter into an agreement to buy a certain quantity of products or services over a particular amount of time. These types of agreements, known as *programs,* save the *sales professionals* a great deal of time, too. These contracts for multiple sales allow the *sales professional* more time to get back out in the field to look for new opportunities, instead of reselling each time.

In the **Closing stage**, turning every *project* into a *program* can help you "Work smarter and not harder". This tactic also will make you and the company more money.

> **KEY TAKEAWAY**
> **Turn every Project into a Program. That's working smarter and not harder!**

Pricing and Price

It is up to a company to make sure that their customers understand the difference between lowest price and best value. Price has been and will always be a crucial subject in any closing situation. I have gone through sales training classes that suggest price doesn't matter and I have read articles by sales experts that say being the vendor with the lowest price doesn't matter. Yes, it does! Has anyone heard of Wal-Mart? Is cost the leading reason customers buy? Not always, but many times, it is!

I will use a B2C – business-to-consumer example. I like Les Schwab tire stores. They do not always have the lowest prices, but they are very competitive. Les Schwab has stores all over the western United States, and if I have any tire problems after the sale, they will fix them for free. To me, the *total cost of ownership* of the tires is less expensive with Les Schwab. Yes, I could get my tires repaired at the other retailers for free. However, there is only one competitor's location in my area. It has limited hours and it is just not convenient.

The point is that I appreciate the true or full value of Les Schwab's service, not just the tires. I have had past personal experiences that reinforced the value. For example, I have had tire problems in other cities and dropped by a Les Schwab tire store for a quick check, free of charge.

I read a great *talk off* to handle the objection of price. "We may not have the lowest price but we are definitely the least costly over time." Sadly, most of the time companies do a poor job of educating their new and existing customers on the *true value* of their products and services

When I worked for Simplex, I utilized *bundling* of products and services to increase the value of my offerings. These were often bid situations, but the *total cost* of doing business with me was lower.

The first thing a company should define is what products and services they have to offer to their customer. Remember, products become commodities quickly. What tangibles and intangibles does your company offer their customers? Make a list! Brainstorm with all your employees to come up with a list! Many companies provide services for free. Unfortunately, their customers don't know about these free services, because they were not told.

When I worked at Kinko's most people would think that a copy is a copy. I would sell all the products and services we offered as a total package. Visibly, there was just a bunch of copies, but what made the package attractive were all the other tangible and intangible services that we sold. There were many different formats; super fast turn around and free delivery to locations all over the United States that made us worth more.

Stressing services that aren't important to the customer is a common mistake made by many *sales professionals.* You have to continually educate the customer on all you offer and stress the parts of your offering that are important to the customer. At Kinko's, if a particular customer never needed to have jobs produced around the county, then stressing that option would not have added to Kinko's total value.

By always using the word "quotes", you are training your customers to think about getting quotes from your competitors. I have worked for several places that tell their customers, "Yes, I can get you a quote." It would be better to say, "I will get you some pricing on the *project* with the tight deadlines as we have discussed." Furthermore, one company I worked for put a slip of colored paper inside every order that read, "We will beat any written quote by another competitor." As a result, we were training our customers that dealing with us was only about price.

It is the job of the *sales professional* to investigate the customer's criteria while putting together pricing. It is also part of the job to help the customer become familiar with other products and services that might be needed to help meet or exceed the customer's criteria. These additional items could be products and services for which your company charges a fee or may provide them at no cost. Onsite support, free delivery, 24/7 online support, contracts/no contracts, anything that the customer would find of value should be part of your service. It is very important that the customer is aware that all of what your company has to offer is part of what they are buying. If your customers truly know what you and your company provides to them, then your company will not be at the higher price, but the best option at the lowest cost.

> ### KEY TAKEAWAY
> **Always stress lowest cost vs. lowest price.**

Pricing Nightmare

The methods many companies use to come up with their pricing are often filled with errors. This is a BIG MISTAKE for many. Additionally, the way companies support their sales force in obtaining proper pricing is one of companies' biggest mistakes.

Tools must be made available to simplify the pricing process for the *sales professionals* or companies need to hire experts at pricing. Furthermore, the pricing experts should be accountable for accurate pricing, not the *sales professionals*. The *sales professional's* main job is to spend time selling, not pricing.

Studies have shown that pricing remains a major challenge in many companies. The problem may be much worse than the studies have shown, because many of the participants in the sales studies are at the sales manager level and above. If the same studies were to survey the average *sales professional*, I think companies would find that pricing is a much bigger challenge to their sales force than the studies have shown. Companies need to decide whether they want their sales force to be experts at pricing or experts at selling.

I have a saying I have used many times in my sales journey:

> **BIG MISTAKE**
> **The easiest part of my job is selling; it is the rest that is the hard part.**

This saying is at the core of one of the biggest mistakes companies make and provides one of the best opportunities to improve sales. The toughest part for any sales force should be the selling part, NOT the **Fulfillment & Support** before and after the sale. If I make a sale and the company doesn't fulfill what has been *promised*, the *sales professional* has succeeded and the company has failed. If the company expects the sales professional to develop accurate pricing, the company is making a BIG MISTAKE. Pricing is not a *revenue-generating activity*. I will cover this saying in detail in the **Fulfillment & Support Strategy stages**.

I have had firsthand experience working for companies where coming up with accurate pricing for products and services was nearly impossible. One of these companies claimed to have pricing experts at the headquarters and a new vice president, as a test, had them try to price a sample job. Not one of the experts came up with the same price. Not only that, they weren't even close to one another.

> **BIG MISTAKE**
> **Expecting sales professionals to be experts at pricing, rather than selling.**

Bringing In Subject Experts & Other Company Resources

As mentioned in the **Prospecting Strategy stage**, I was successful at utilizing subject experts to gain more appointments. Subject experts also helped me (**Closing Strategy stage**) to close more business.

Subject experts, managers or higher ups in companies are valuable resources, but they have to be used correctly or their incorrect use can cost the company substantial amounts of money.

For example, when I worked for Collection Bureau, Inc., I would bring in Mark Clark, an attorney, with over 30 years experience. I would sell the meeting to the prospect by saying I was bringing in my boss as resource and I would explain that his expertise would bring great value to the customer. The important next step is that each knows his role in the meeting. If you have a domineering manager, remind him or her to include you in the conversation. You might even coach him to say at some particular point in the meeting, "This is where, (insert *sales professional's* name), has the most expertise," thus giving credibility to the *sales professional*.

The *sales professional's* expertise could come from having met with numerous businesses and discovering best practices that may help the prospect to avoid similar mistakes.

At Intermountain Technology Group, I would bring in a subject expert and remind the customer that my task was to make sure that the right resources were brought to the table to enable them to handle their challenges and to be more competitive.

This technique of bringing in subject experts and additional resources can be very successful in showing the value of doing business with you. Companies are starting to understand that with the complexity of some of today's solutions; it is becoming customary to have to bring in additional expertise to close new business.

Do Not Give Away Your Expertise and Time

A discovery that I made years ago is that you have to be careful not to give away your expertise and time for free to customers, especially prospective customers.

Many well intentioned *sales professionals* will bring in additional resources, help the customer identify the problems; come up with solutions and a cost for your company to solve their problems. All for free! What a BIG MISTAKE! The more complex the sale, the easier it is for a *sales professional* and their company to get caught up in giving away their expertise for free.

> **BIG MISTAKE**
> **Giving away your expertise and time for free.**

A good example would be going to a doctor. She will listen to your problems, to diagnose your ailment and then send you to a specialist. Does all this happen for free? Of course not, you get charged for both doctors' expertise.

Why don't *sales professionals* look at themselves the same way? You are experts who are bringing in other experts/resources. You need to be paid for your time and expertise.

Senior Grandmaster Ed Parker used to tell a story at his seminars about a company that had an important piece of equipment that stopped working. This equipment was vital and had to be fixed. The company called in an expert, who did about one-half hour's worth of checking out the equipment and then hit it with a large hammer. The equipment started working again as if nothing was ever wrong and the owner was ecstatic that it was fixed so quickly.

Then, the owner received a bill for $900. The owner and expert ended up going to court over this charge and the judge found in favor of the expert. The expert had charged $100 for a site visit and $800 for knowing where to hit the equipment to make it start working again.

This story makes a great point that many companies and their sales forces need to consider. Understand that your expertise is the difference you bring to the table for the customer. You are getting paid for knowing "how" and "why" and not always for "what" you do. "Here, Mr. Customer, I will do all the work, diagnose your problem, come up with solutions and put it all in a nice orderly list so you can send it to my competitors for the lowest price." And their price is lower because they have little or no investment to cover, since I did all the work.

After having been taken advantage of by a prospective customer, I have learned several ways to make the customers pay for the expertise and resources I bring to the table. While working for Simplex as a Service *Sales Professional*, I would convince a prospect that Simplex should do some sort of testing and maintenance of their fire system. If there were no documentation of fire alarm equipment for a building or buildings, I would have to do a physical survey of them.

These surveys used a significant amount of my time. I would then set up a meeting using my *Good, Better, Best* technique and a list of all the types and quantities of equipment. One of my prospects took my equipment list and proposal and faxed it to a competitor to get a price comparison. Wow! I felt betrayed. I had made several mistakes. The biggest was giving away my time for free.

What is important is that I learned from my mistakes and used the knowledge in every other position I have held in my sales journey.

At Simplex, none of my future proposals included device counts. I just featured types and a total cost. It appeared that our competitors would simply guess on the qualities and usually estimate on the high side to cover themselves. Occasionally, I had customers ask me why I didn't include the quantities and I would tell them that my survey would not be as accurate as our certified technicians would supply (after we got the order). If the technicians found any additional types or models of devices, the additional devices would be tested and documented at no additional cost, just as another thanks for their business. This tactic worked very well.

Occasionally, a prospective customer would try to push for the list before they had committed to contract with Simplex. At such times, I would tell them that my consulting and surveys are all provided at no charge up front and are part of our services, but they could not be provided for free. This tactic also worked very well. My competitor at the time did not want to take the time up front to survey, which gave Simplex and me a strategic advantage.

The same technique worked well when I was in the Simplex building systems division. There were often long hours spent on reviewing blue prints, counting devices, reading specifications and designing the right panel configuration.

Some electrical contractors would want a detailed list of equipment, devices and their costs. Several times, I would have to use the same *talk offs* as I did in the Service Sales division. I would explain all the expertise and time put into developing my price and that I could not afford to give it to my competitors for free. We offer it for no charge to the customer, after commitment, but never for free to competitors. Expertise and time are parts of the total cost and customers must be reminded if you are pushed.

While working for ITG, Intermountain Technology Group, I was very careful to follow the MSA methodology and to learn from my mistakes in order to continue improving. I would have a prospect acknowledge that they had to start looking into some solutions for problems or potential problems regarding their computer network.

I might bring in a subject expert in the initial stages of the sale cycle, but if the customer wanted to know what size hammer and where to hit their problem, it was going to cost them. I would have our IT experts put together a discovery which was a plan of action, step by step, with timelines of who was responsible for what, (customer or ITG) and a total cost for the *project* or *program*. This was like what a doctor does. The patient tells them they have a problem. The doctor does a thorough diagnosis of the problem and the patient is charged for the diagnosis. I did the same. My thorough diagnosis was called a "discovery" and it worked.

Before I was employed by ITG, many others in the company did the discoveries for no charge. I always charged for the discovery. Our experts would diagnose the problems, just like a doctor and my customers knew that they would be charged for that expertise.

Once the discovery was completed I would put together an itemized scope letter with all the work that had to be completed and the equipment needed. Scope letters are typically like a resume, with one or two pages of all the highlights. They are detailed overviews of setting up the mutually agreed upon *promise*: what has my company agreed or *promised* to provide to the customer in return for a certain amount of money? My goal was to provide service, which was at a higher margin than the equipment, usually sold at a lower margin. As everyone knows, IT/network equipment is very competitively priced; but, in these situations, I could make a little money on the equipment because I used the *bundling* technique for the whole *project*. I never provided a detailed list of equipment numbers. Doing so would make it easy for a competitor to avoid spending any time or resources to analyze and diagnose the customer's problems. Since our experts would have already spent time properly configuring the equipment needed to fix the customer's problems, all a competitor would have to do is to look up prices from our equipment list and provide his bid.

I would include an equipment list without manufacturers' numbers and the configurations of the equipment. My guarantee was that we would provide the proper configuration of the equipment to help the prospect with the problems we uncovered.

I never gouged my customers because I would lose trust with the customer if discovered. My customers were going to get a great value to solve their problems, not necessarily the lowest price on their service and equipment.

For on-going *programs*, well written SLA's, Service Level Agreements should be put into place. SLA's work well to remind everyone of the details of the agreement. A well written SLA is very important because it reminds the customer of exactly what is expected for products and services.

When I worked for Kinko's, I would make up a sample of the product the customer was interested in. This would allow me to show the customer the quality of our products and, of course, the service. Getting the resources together in a very quick manner to provide a sample of the upcoming *project* would impress the customer and many times they would ask for a price. This then would open up a discussion of *projects* and *programs*. How often did they run these? Why? Quantities needed each run? If it were a recurring order, then I would explain how they could run them less often, making it easier to update changes. I would turn such jobs into "print on demand", print only as many as needed. This was Kinko's strength, providing smaller quantities with a fast turnaround and less inventory costs. Then, I would explain to prospects that if they would let Kinko's be responsible for a year's worth, I could give them a *program* cost, where volume allowed for discounting the price. When I gave them the costs, it would not be a detailed list of everything line by line to make it easy for a competitor to take my work and give a quote. I would include any tight timelines, free delivery, times of delivery and digital imaging, all of which were all our strengths. This tactic would accomplish two main things. It would make it more difficult for the customer simply to fax a detailed quote to a competitor, and often the customer would feel indebted to me for my help and hustle. This feeling of indebtedness would provide opportunities to prove myself on their next *project*. This often leads to a *program*, with the customers reordering the same job over and over again.

Companies and *sales professionals* need to be diligent not to give away their time and expertise for FREE. It is the company's and *sales professional's* job to make sure this does not happen by obtaining upfront verbal and written commitments from their prospects and customers. Also, it is their job to educate both prospects and customers that there is a cost for their time and expertise. Thus, there is a need for "a commitment to buy".

Closing Strategies and Techniques

Closing techniques have been available forever. Many of them haven't changed that much, but the *set up* and *approach* has changed because the business environment is so much different than a few years ago.

Many closing techniques have to be adapted to be industry specific. Let's cover the methods that are most universal. Closing skills are analogous to the "finishing moves" of the mixed martial arts (MMA). You can talk forever and circle the opponent endlessly, but you have to get the customer to commit or the rest is in vain.

I have given B2C – business-to-consumer examples, because they tend to be the easiest to identify for the largest audience. However, it is necessary for companies and the sale forces to understand fully the difference between B2C and B2B. I have always been in B2B sales and would only solicit B2C sales for a strategic reason, such as to gain favor with a key customer. I would never simply solicit a B2C sale without a definite reason. Not knowing the difference can set a company and its sales force up for failure.

Assumptive Close

One example of an aged closing technique is asking a leading question, "What color do you like best?" "Would you like it in red or blue?" or "Would you like it delivered Monday or Friday?" These closes have been around forever and are still successful. They are examples of assumptive closes. The *sales professional* is using language that assumes that the customer has already committed to buy. This tactic usually helps the *sales professional* to find out quickly if the customer is thinking of buying or still undecided.

I have used the assumptive closes in many different closing situations, and I have used variations of the following numerous times:

"Sounds like our companies are a good fit, what are the *next steps*?"

"All I need to do now is put together the final scope letter with your timeline. It sounds like we are going to make you look good."

Stronger: "When would you want me to schedule the first technician site visit?"

"In order for me to meet your tight timeline I will need a written commitment signed by the end of the week."

Buying Signals

I consider myself a pretty good closer, and I am always striving to become better to "Increase My Odds".

Buying signals appear when the prospective customer starts asking questions, such as:

"How much does it cost?"
"How long would it take to finish?"
"How fast can you deliver it?"
"Who else have you helped with this?"
...and the best:
"How would we get started"?

In order to recognize this golden moment, the *sales professional* needs to be listening very carefully for one of these verbal gifts.

Jeffrey Gitomer, a best-selling sales author and expert, writes for many publications and has some very useful ideas on the assumptive close. He asks confirming questions for the assumptive close. If the customer says, "Can you deliver it by next week?" Jeffrey Gitomer recommends then asking a confirming question in response; "Do you need it by next week?" This is an excellent tactic and just shows that if a company is following the MSA methodology, they easily can add this great idea to improve their closing technique of assumptive closes.

One of the strengths I have and every *sales professional* needs is to know when to ask for the order and then to do it. This loaded question is not always presented in a direct way, but it usually contains an assumptive close. Two of my standards are, "When do you want to start?" and "When do you think it would be best to ship the first order?"

Many *sales professionals* just keep talking small talk; and worse yet, set up another meeting. This is a huge waste, especially since the opening was right there and fatally ignored. Then, the prospective customer usually says the dreaded, "Let me think about it some more.", "I have been so busy and I will call you back when things settle down." Many of the prospective customers could have said, "OK, let's get it going." Now, having missed the closing signal and not reacted to it, the *sales professional* faces a loss. By the time the prospect receives the call back, the urgency has died down and they frequently won't even return your calls.

> **KEY TAKEAWAY**
>
> **"Don't confuse effort with results!"**
>
> **Richard Marker, My dad, fighter pilot, retired**
> **Air Force Lieutenant Colonel, engineer**

Just as in an MMA match, you need to recognize the opportunity to finish, close the deal and end the fight. Many MMA competitors have been so close to finishing the fight, only to back off and let their opponent regroup and come back to win.

When I worked for Simplex in the Time and Attendance division, one of our senior technicians told me that I got the most orders for projects because I asked for the order, "When would you like to start?" He said that the other *sales professionals* he made sales calls with never asked for the order or for a commitment to get started. I never considered myself a hard closer, but I did try to close with an assumptive close or test close. Not all customers are going to tell you, "OK, you have sold me, let's get going". I have had it happen; but, if I had waited every time, I would have gone broke. To *increase your odds* you have to try to close. The worst the prospective customer can do is say "NO", or ask more questions. Either case is a step closer to the final close or your exit cue to move on to the next opportunity.

Who Else is Involved in the Final Approval?

This is a great probing and closing question. Remember, "It isn't what you say but how you say it." It is best not to say, "Are you the decision maker?" This might not be the person who has the authority to sign the purchase order, but she might be the person with the final authority to allow you a chance to gain the opportunity. Your contact may be a valuable sponsor to help you sell your company's products and services to the final decision maker. Although your contact might not have the authority to sign the final approval, she really may be the decision maker and her boss's responsibility is to act on her recommendations.

It is much better to ask, "Who else is involved?", because if the person you are talking to is obviously involved, you do not want to insult or exclude them. By asking who else is involved helps you know if this contact is the last person you have to convince to close the deal. Asking this question also can protect you from getting blind-sided right at the end of your closing. Normally, the larger the opportunity, the more people who will be involved in the final approval. Ask in order to be safe and sure.

Order Starters

Low cost *order starters "lower the risk"* for the customer to give your company a try. Many companies will even give out a free sample of their product to *lower the risk* and make it easy for a customer to try them out before committing. *Order starters* can help you get your foot in the door.

This has been a very effective closing technique for me. When I worked for Trend/Westcoast, our sales force called specific items *order starters*. We would have a cool, inexpensive item that many times the customer would buy because it was at a very low cost. This was a type of impulse buy. It would get customers in the ordering mood and very often turn into additional items being purchased. I would be sure to mention that there was a minimum amount to be ordered before the shipping would be at no charge. Once they ordered my *order starter* item, customers generally would continue to order until they reached the minimum order quantity for free shipping.

Many times the customer would start off the conversation by saying "We didn't need anything at this time". By having an *order starter*, I could always just say that I have one cool thing they have to check out. It worked more times than not. This is a perfect example of where people "love to buy" but don't always like to be sold.

I also used this technique very successfully at Kinko's. Typically, I would try to get a *project*. My goal was to get any order to prove myself, and an *order starter* was very useful in accomplishing this objective. Then, I worked hard to impress the customer on that first job, no matter how small. Often, the small order would lead to another order and then to other opportunities.

At Kinko's, I had a customer who placed many little orders and I asked him if there was a goal to all the small orders. He told me the goal was to roll out the finished items to their 1,400 locations across the county. That large *project* was a direct result of *order starters* that proved my company's capabilities. I worked closely with him for a couple of months.

Many times, I would get that first order which would lead to a *program* and we would run that particular item in larger quantities on an ongoing basis. Developing or acquiring such *programs* is always my long-term strategic goal. The first objective is to get the customer to give me a chance. With a new customer, there is a very low probability that I can win an opportunity at a *program* or a large *program* without proving myself first. This I do with an *order starter*.

Cross-Selling and Up-Selling

All *sales professionals* need to be trained to look for cross-selling and up-selling opportunities. Cross-selling is where you try to get a customer to buy additional items in the same type of product or service. This can occur when the customer agrees to carry more sizes of a product or similar items in another line of your company's products. For example, when I represented a beauty supply company, I always tried to get a customer to carry all of our lines of shampoo.

Up-selling is a technique of trying to gain a larger portion of the customer's wallet. This can be accomplished by selling the more expensive, enhanced version or an upgrade of your product, service or solution.

My sales manager at Warner Lambert always stressed up-selling. Not only convincing a customer to carry our products but also to buy supporting displays of those same products. Additionally, he trained us to cross-sell by trying to get customers to increase the number of different products we offered and to carry the full line sizes of each product. As a result of these efforts, we dominated most of the shelf space in most of our stores. Our district sales force was always at the top or near the top of the list of the company's sales forces across the United States.

When I worked for Simplex and *bundled* several products and services together, this was creative cross-selling and up-selling. Moreover, when I was working as a building systems sales representative, I sold zone and addressable fire alarm systems. Zone systems were entry level and only would notify of an area in trouble, a problem with a device or if there was an alarm. An addressable system would notify the exact location of a device in trouble or an alarm. Each device had a unique, individual address, making it much easier to find and troubleshoot problems. The addressable systems were substantially easier to maintain, but there was an upfront increase in cost. I always tried to sell addressable systems. They were more expensive but the best value for an owner, because there was a *lower cost of ownership* over the life of the system.

Studies show that almost fifty percent of respondents surveyed rated their sales forces as needing improvement in both cross-selling and up-selling. Companies need to arm their sales forces with best practices and to continually exchange successful strategies and techniques for success on up/cross-selling.

Lower Cost of Ownership

As just described, addressable fire alarm maintenance costs were substantially less over the life of the fire alarm system. However, it is human nature to look only at the immediate lower cost. It is the *sales professional's* job to educate the customer to look at the *total cost of ownership* over time. If the fire alarm typically lasts eight to ten years, for example, how much would each type of system cost over its lifetime? The drastic difference must also be explained. Problems with peripheral devices, pull stations and smoke detectors are much more difficult to find in a zone system. As its name implies, an addressable system is much easier to maintain and a building owner can cut down on false alarms which frustrate tenants. Minimizing the frustration of tenants is a goal of most building owners. False alarms make owning a fire alarm system a constant problem. By spending a little more money up front, building owners can avoid lots of *pain* in dealing with false alarms and higher maintenance cost for the life of the fire alarm system. Using these facts, I persuaded or up-sold most of my customers to buy addressable systems. I wasn't selling a piece of equipment but a "solution" for reducing both costs and headaches to building owners.

Company Tour - Prospects and Customers Come To Visit

The tactic of bringing a customer to your business for a tour can be used to close new business or to reinforce the relationship with an existing customer. This is a very powerful tool if done correctly. As with any other sales presentation, it has to be a balance of education and entertainment.

When I worked at Kinko's, I followed the example set by another *sales professional.* We only offered these tours to high-potential prospective customers or good, existing customers. This was done, because setting up a tour required much time and work if it was to be successful. With a lot of help from the inside *sales professional,* I would put together a very entertaining and educational walk through. There would be a custom welcome sign when they entered the Kinko's branch. Then, we began where many of the orders would be emailed to us. We explained the Kinko's system and I would interject, "You all better pay attention, because there will be valuable prizes for those who do pay attention." Then, as we left the first department, I would ask a question about something I had just covered. Someone would answer the question and I would say, "You are correct" and give them a free ticket to a local movie theater. Everyone would laugh, but after that, everyone paid closer attention. I continued to ask a question at the end of each department and it became fun because almost everyone would try to answer the question. The inside *sales professional* did a great job of providing a lot of extras. In the binding department, she would have samples of several types of our bindings with the customer's company logo on the front of each sample. These little touches really impressed our visitors. I would hear over and over again, "Wow, I just didn't know you could do all these different things." We had personnel from many different customer departments show up for the tour, and the tour gave both Kinko's and me more exposure with the customers.

I would end the tour in a room with box lunches from a great sandwich shop. Inside each box were some fun prizes: pens, note pads and one of the boxes would have two movie passes in it. These tours were hugely successful. They did take time, so I was careful only to bring in customers with large potential. Customers talked about the tours for months and even years afterwards, so our business-to-business relationships were expanded and maintained.

Any customer tour needs to be educational, entertaining and not boring. You have to make it an event they will remember you by.

Who else are you talking to?

If you have not figured out whether your prospective customer is also talking to a competitor and you suspect that they are, then I recommend you ask, "Who else are you talking to about this project?" If they are also talking to a competitor and if they divulge who it is, then this information helps you to strategize your closing points to highlight your company's strengths and bring to light your competitor's weaknesses. As I stated before, never bad mouth the competition but structure your presentation to highlight the advantages in doing business with you.

I have had customers ask me what I think of a competitor and I always said, "They have something to offer. However, many of my customers and I feel that my company offers the best total package, i.e., the best value for our customers."

Formal and Informal Proposals

I have the most experience with informal proposals, which are usually short, highlight my company's strengths and cover all mutually agreed upon requirements. I try to keep them short but concise.

Furthermore, I believe in establishing the expectations clearly before you both commit. Too many *sales professionals* rush to get the order with little thought of what they have agreed to provide to the customer. If the customer expects a lot more than what was agreed upon, it can prove to be very costly to the *sales professional* and the company. The best way to avoid such a negative situation is to set realistic expectations. "Under promise and over perform" has always been the best practice for me. It is much easier to exceed the customer's expectations when you set the bar low. I did this in many ways: delivering products early, beating deadlines and performing better than agreed upon.

When selling complex deals or products and services with deadlines, I would write a "scope letter", with assistance from our subject experts. These were not required but helped both the customer and the company remember what had been agreed upon. There have been several times in my experience that having it in writing "saved my butt". These occurrences took place with customers who got amnesia or when my original contact had left the company and I found myself with a new contact questioning our agreement. More than once, I had to remind my own company of the details of an agreement. It is much easier to avoid or to handle this problem by reviewing a mutually agreed upon and mutually signed scope letter.

Taking the time to write up a scope letter helps prevent what I call "scope creep". Scope creep happens when your customer keeps asking for more than was specified and your company obliges by providing more services and products, because there were never any clear goals or a defined end to the project. A good scope letter helps avoid this kind of problem and the dreaded "scope creep".

I have found that getting something in writing signed by both the customer and your company's representative is a *Truth*, otherwise known as a best practice.

KEY TAKEAWAY

Under promising and over performing is a great strategy for any sales professional.

Formal proposals can be very time consuming and costly to both *sales professionals* and their companies. Since these proposals can consume a great deal of time and resources, the *sales professional* and the company need to qualify the opportunity. Ask the prospect or customer questions up front: After you give them the proposal, what are the *next steps*? What are the timelines and how does the approval process work? That way, you know what to expect. I don't recommend spending your time and the company's resources putting together a formal proposal without getting answers to lots of questions upfront. I tell the customer that I am willing to spend the time to put together a custom proposal for their benefit but that I will need some type of commitment that my time will be rewarded if it satisfies their questions. If someone tells you they have no budget, no timeline and just want to know what is out there, you need to decide if it is worth your time to proceed. Explain that you are willing to put in the time and expense to earn their business but that you need some type of commitment that the prospects are going to take action if you make a good business case to proceed. I have given customers rough verbal estimates. This has more than once saved me from a lot of work.

Additionally, companies need to assist their *sales professional* in the writing of any formal proposals. I have found that the most successful proposals that lead to a sale come from companies which provide proposal templates and/or management assistance in writing, developing and reviewing proposals. It is not always the best use of a *sales professional's* time to write up a formal proposal, and companies need to make it a priority to assist their *sales professionals* in developing and producing formal proposals so that they have a high probability of success.

Proposals should focus on the prospective customer's specific needs, not on what your company thinks is most important. How much will they save, how much will it reduce downtime, overtime, etc? If your company typically can save a customer ten percent, then try to find out what dollar amount it will equate to the prospective customer in savings the first year. This type of detailing is very personal, persuasive and powerful in a proposal. Prospects' hot buttons should always be included.

I included such particulars many times when I worked for Simplex in their Time and Attendance division. Utilizing an American Payroll Association study percentage, I would equate the cost savings using the percentage quoted from the association and the number I received from the customer to come up with a total savings dollar figure. Now, it was real and personal, not just a national survey percentage, and I had done the numbers for them.

RFP - Request for Proposal, RFB - Request for Bid, RFI - Request for Information are not usually the best procedures for *sales professionals* to show their company's value. Consequently, I have always worked hard to try to get opportunities removed from the bid arena. Historically, these requests are all about the lowest price. Price should not be the only factor in determining the winner, and many of the government agencies are now allowed to use several factors to determine the winning vendor. This is an improvement, but it is still very challenging to highlight the strengths and total value of your company. As a *sales professional*, you at least want your expertise, help, service, etc, to be worth a little higher price. Sometimes though, you have to be creative and following are a few examples of my experiences.

If there is a RFP, RFB, or RFI, I quickly evaluate the opportunity. These formalities can be very time consuming and you may have a lower than normal chance of success. Many companies and *sales professionals* waste a lot of their valuable time and company's resources chasing "low-percentage" and low margin opportunities.

If you and your company evaluate the opportunity as something that is worth your time, then you have to be strategic in your *approach*. I have worked for companies that had whole departments specializing in replying to bid requests, especially government ones. Using company bidding specialists increases your chances of getting a piece of the huge government business out there. Remember though, is this opportunity a good fit? Is it going to be a *project* or *program*? Is your company set up to properly respond to these Requests For...? A lot of questions must be answered before your time and your company's resources are invested.

When replying to a Request For..., I always read it very carefully.

Most are very long and detailed. Many times, it is difficult to determine what they really want or what their goal is. After reading and marking some questions, I always call the main contact. First, if I have other contacts who can give me additional information, I start with them first. This is similar to the **Prospecting Strategy stage**. Other contacts may give critical information, such as why they are looking to change, which competitors they have used before, and/or what their success or failure experience was. These points are all very critical in writing your response to the Request For.... Is the bid request slanted to favor a particular competitor? I have challenged certain requirements successfully, citing why they aren't needed or how my company can accomplish the same result with a different feature.

Next, I call the main contact and try to set up a meeting. Today, most government agencies won't meet with you because they don't want to have to meet with all the other vendors responding to the Requests For.... The government contacts will usually have you email your questions to them. Then, they are answered and posted for all vendors to see the responses.

This is why it is critical to get involved with a government contact, just as in the private sector, before and while the Request For... is being crafted.

At Simplex, I would be working with a customer who told me that they were required to put the *project* out for bid out. I would help them design the systems needs and provide specification outlines to be included in the bids. These specifications were general but did favor my systems' strengths. This assistance alone saved my contacts hours of research and work. I would also "sell" to the customer that reliable, local service was imperative, and they might put in the specifications that the servicing had to be local. This requirement eliminated many of my competitors. I really did feel that the specifications I recommended were in their best interest, so I could be passionate about the importance of certain features.

Your contacts look to you for your expertise. Try to be balanced in your *approach*. Do not be overzealous and don't think that you are going to convince them that your company is the only company that can satisfy their needs. It is best to convince them that your company would be the best option, not the only option for their requirements.

Also, I would list the value of services that we provided free of charge if not required by the bid. Twenty four hour emergency service, local factory trained and certified support technicians and local stocking of critical equipment spare parts were always good to include. Little things your company might provide for free and doesn't realize increases the value, e.g., additional equipment manual, which cost $15 each, will be free with the contract. The point is that companies give away products and services without getting credit for them. All I was doing was putting a value on our giveaways.

Also, find out how much the government prospect is allowed to purchase from you without having to go to bid. I made a number of sales to government agencies armed with *intelligence*. I have established relationships with contacts who have had a $500 limit but were sponsors who then talked to contacts several levels above them who had a $10,000 limit before having to request bids. This type of information is critical. The keys here are to build as many relationships as possible and to find out if your contacts can purchase products and services under a certain amount without bidding.

At Simplex I would have testing agreements for a building with our equipment, and often the contact would think it just made sense to have the manufacturer continue the maintenance. I could get an agreement without having the purchase go to bid, because the cost was under the allowable amount for that particular government contact. This helped me get paid for all the time and expertise I brought to the table.

When responding to "Requests For...", write your proposal by exactly following the procedure and order of items in the "Request For...." If, for example, the first page is a form to fill out with your company contact information, then that is exactly what the first page of your proposal must be. If you add anything, add it at the end of the appropriate section, in the same order as the Request For....

Remember, whether in the private or public sector, "Make it easy to buy and easy to do business with" is a huge means of increasing your sales!

The bottom line is that putting it in writing is a best practice. It is a *Universal Truth*. Whether there is an informal proposal or a formal proposal, it is important to put it in writing and to be concise and persuasive. Writing great proposals is becoming a science. Many companies would be best advised to consult a subject expert. In the mixed martial arts, a particular team will bring in an expert in a particular discipline such as grappling, striking, takedowns, conditioning or nutrition. The same should be done from time to time in the *mixed selling arts* world.

There are companies which are experts in particular aspects of sales. One such company that specializes in proposal writing which I have been impressed with is The Sant Corporation at www.santcorp. com.

Presentations

Presentations should be like doing a traditional martial arts form (American name)/kata (original name). They are a preset, solo and choreographed sequence of moves, i.e., stances, blocks and strikes as in martial arts competitions. You want to begin with explosive movements to gain the audience's immediate attention.

When I competed in traditional martial arts tournament competitions, I followed the lead of Professor Hancock, my Kenpo Instructor. He would even bow into the ring explosively, which immediately gained the judges' attention. Then, he would proceed through his routine with a mixture of smooth and quick explosive moves. He was using *broken rhythm* in his forms/kata competitions, by changing the pace and tempo intermittently to keep it exciting and to hold the judges' attention.

I have followed his advice and expanded on his lead. I have told my students that the competition starts the second you arrive at the event. It doesn't matter if you are competing in fighting, weapons, forms/ kata or the self-defense divisions. During the whole day of the event, your actions influence spectators and, most importantly, the potential judges.

It is important to be respectful and to show confidence while waiting your turn to compete. I teach my students to be *aware* of themselves and their *environment*. Standing around talking and acting unprofessional, can and does influence the judges.

I also tried to end explosively, to make sure I ended with a bang. This tactic helps the judges remember me. I have judged traditional competitions in the martial arts and after a while many of the routines start to become a blur. As a competitor, you have to help the judges remember you. Being crisp and clean with a great start and ending will help you impress the judges.

Doing a form/kata with lots of detail is important but it is like a presentation. The ones having only a bunch of information and features will not be the most successful. Your goal is to be informative, but most importantly, in either the *MSA* world or the MMA world, be persuasive. Using *broken rhythm* and moving at a steady pace with pauses mixed in, helps create a most exciting presentation. In the sales world, *broken rhythm* is crucial. Mixing up the tempo of a verbal presentation while adding pauses helps hold the audience's attention.

In traditional martial arts forms I used to use "kiai", a shout to help accentuate the effects. In the business world, it is best not to shout but to ask prospects or customers questions at the beginning and throughout the presentation. These questions keep the audience on their toes.

Presentations need to start off getting your audience's attention and then holding it with a mixture of entertainment, information and persuasion. You are trying to convince your audience that they need to choose your company. In martial arts, you need to end with something that will help them remember you and persuade them to give you the high score. In business, even paced presentations will begin to bore your audience and make you seem like every other competitor before you.

Handing out a company's own figures is much more powerful than using generic figures derived from other companies. Also, to get your audience's attention, begin by stating a company's challenges and a quick story of how you helped another company with similar problems. Having letters of recommendation on top of the information you hand out helps to build your credibility.

Knowing your audience is extremely helpful and important. Is your audience made up of CXO's?, mid-management? or even a mix? Typically, each level has different priorities. Some levels are more prone to care about making themselves look good and making their job easier. While some levels care about making themselves look good but also care more about saving the company money and increasing profits. Other levels seem to care about reducing losses and increasing revenues to make themselves look good. Again, knowing your audience is very important.

When I competed in traditional karate tournaments, I used to look at the judges (their patches and uniforms identified their style preferences), and depending on their style, I would change my kata/ form slightly to better influence them and benefit my scores.

In the sales world, you also have to be *aware* of your *environment.* Depending on the types of people in the audience, I will change the way I do my presentation. It is also helpful to learn from any previous meetings you have had with others in the company, because you pick up keys to their company's culture and terminology from those meetings. Then, you can tailor your presentation to the company's particular likes and dislikes.

All *sales professionals* need to do the same in all presentations. Start with a bang, end with a bang, use *broken rhythm* and any former *intelligence*, and most importantly, focus on persuasion over features. Your main goal is to persuade them to take "Action"!

Additionally, an MMA competitor would never go into a championship match out of shape. That would be disastrous. Similarly, a *sales professional* should always, be prepared before giving a presentation.

Objections and Rejections

Although there have been volumes of books written on this subject, here are some nuggets of wisdom from the trenches. Practice, rehearse and practice and rehearse some more. Practice out loud at least and in front of others if at all possible. On countless occasions, I was able to handle an objection just because I learned from the same objection raised at a previous sales opportunity.

If you do not know the answer, tell the prospect or customer you do not know the answer but that you will find out and get back to them. Then, make it a point to get back to them with the answer. Two things will happen. You will build credibility by following up and not having tried to fake it or attempting to lie. And once you find the answer, you're ready for the next time you are asked that question or get that objection. Also, exchanging stories with other *sales professionals* of overcoming objections can be very helpful. Remember, constantly learning is a critical part of the game.

A great way to overcome an objection is to begin by agreeing with the prospect, "That is a concern but other clients have found the benefits far outweigh the drawbacks". When practicing grappling there are a handful of attacks that you have to defend against 80 percent of the time. Knowing these common attacks helps you be more perceptive, so you don't get into those positions of vulnerability.

In sales, there are many objections that are common to all industries and other objections that will be more industry specific. Remember, always be prepared. Know that handful of objections before you get in front of the customer and prepare for them. Structure your presentations to try to overcome the objections before they even come up. Objections are like submissions in the mixed martial arts world; it is better to try to prevent them before they happen. Moreover, having well crafted stories and references help eliminate many objections up front.

All *sales professionals* know that you cannot prevent all the objections. "Your price is too high", is a very common objection. At such a time, you could mention that one of the customers who wrote one of your letters of recommendation had the same thought at first: but, you can relate that they discovered that the total value far exceeded the price. Structure your stories to mention that many of your customers found they were saving large amounts of money annually. Going on the offense to help overcome probable objections while you are presenting is always better than going on the defensive.

"The budget has been cut!" If you didn't or couldn't build a good enough case for this objection, then you need to be ready, in advance, with questions that will help overcome the objection. "When will the budget be restored?" "Is there enough to start the project if we split the payments over the next four quarters?"

"Your price is higher than the other vendor." Respond with, "Did you know our product lasts up to four times longer? Because of that we are slightly higher in price but the total value is also substantially higher!" Always be prepared.

No matter how prepared you are, you won't have eliminated all the objections. When objections start to become very common, companies need to arm their sales forces with *talk offs*. In the martial arts, they are called "counters" to the common situations. SellingPower.com ran a poll on the most common objections that *sales professionals* encounter. Companies need to prepare sales forces to be ready to handle the objections or be ready to lose a lot of sales.

The poll results were very familiar to me and I am sure to many *sales professionals*:

1. Need to think about it
2. Price too high
3. Happy with current supplier
4. Waiting for the economy to pick up
5. Need to get approval
6. Considering other vendors

Others that are common:

1. No budget
2. Send me a proposal

3. Not interested
4. Other vendor is cheaper
5. I can get it online
6. Your company isn't big enough
7. Your company is too big,
   and on and on....

How would you overcome these objections? Let's look at one: "We are happy with our current vendor." You need to brainstorm with others. Have any on your sales force been able to overcome that objection? One way I have overcome that same objection is to say, "Let me be a backup if your current vendor can't meet your needs and deadlines". Using this tactic, I have subsequently gotten my foot in the door when another vendor was not able to meet a deadline. When the customer called to see if I could help them out, I not only got the one order but also have impressed the customer enough to become an equal or even the main supplier for that company. The key is that I was ready for my prospect's objection and had a strong response to handle it.

"Let me think it over" is a very common objection. How can you ever overcome that objection and not sound pushy? Well, remember that I have said before, "It isn't what you say but how you say it". I asked the customer what their top two concerns are that they will be thinking over. I have tried to ask this question in a concerned, nice manner because I will bring other information to address those concerns, or better yet, give them a name of another long time customer who initially had those same concerns.

Remember, companies first need to create a framework for their sales processes and then personalize part of the process to take into consideration individuals' styles. I might not be comfortable using a certain *talk off*, but slightly changing the wording might be more effective for my personal style. It is very important to have and to practice strategies, techniques and *talk offs* to overcome objections effectively.

Companies and their sales forces need to come up with a list of the top objections and drill on ways to overcome them. That is what is done in the MMA and that is what should be done in the *MSA*. Most objections are very common and companies and their sales teams need constantly to survey their sales forces for objections they encounter, so they can come up with new ways to overcome them. Making adjustments is a big part of the successful *MSA* game.

The top objections may not always change that much, but the way you overcome them can constantly improve. Constantly refine the *basics, sophisticated basics*!

Never Give Away, but Trade

Here is a challenging scenario: The *sales professional* is ecstatic because the customer tells him that they will go with his company, but there is something they want in exchange.

This is a very common tactic by customers and especially buyers in companies: Customers sometimes will try to strong-arm *sales professionals* into giving up something to get the order. A lower price is a common demand. It is their job to get the best deal, so why wouldn't they ask for a lower price?

I have learned to trade instead of giving away a lower price just to get the order. Remember, the "professional" part of your *sales professional* title. I am a professional and I always try to negotiate or trade with the customer. If they want a lower price at the last minute, that is great. If they commit to a larger quantity or a longer time commitment, I am sure my company will be happy to give them a lower price for their loyalty.

Sales professionals should never just "cave in" and lower their price without getting something from the customer in return. I have used this technique for years and not only has it helped me reap more sales but it gains the respect of many of my customers.

KEY TAKEAWAY
Never give away lower pricing without trading for a valuable commitment from the customer.

Never decide for the customer

One piece of wisdom that I learned from one of my sales managers at Warner Lambert was never to decide for the customer. We would have continual promotions on new products and new product sizes. At times I would think that a certain customer would not want a certain new item or promotion and my sales manager told me, "Never decide for the customer. It is like the saying, never assume. Always make it a point to show the customer all that you have to offer. Frequently, I have been surprised that the customer has bought what I had considered not even showing them. This would have been a BIG MISTAKE!

> **BIG MISTAKE**
> **Never decide for the customer. That decision could cost you a sale.**

Pre-Call & Post-Call reviews

I must stress here the critical importance of both pre-call and post-call reviews in "increasing your odds" for more closes. *Sales professionals* need to plan and strategize before they get in front of a prospect and then do it again after the sales call or presentation. "What am I going to say and stress in the meeting?" Then, after the call, "How did it go? What are the *next steps*? What could we have done better or differently? What can we do next time?"

It is vital that there be brainstorming before and after each sales call, especially if it is a team call.

In the mixed martial arts, the overwhelming majority of competitors plan before a fight. Then, win or lose, they review what went right and what they could have done differently.

Top Down Closing?

As I mentioned in the **Prospecting Strategy stage**, going right to the top to close some new business isn't always the best strategy. Studies have backed up my personal experience. Usually, you must convince a contact at a lower level of the company first, either by earning the company's trust by use of an *order starter* or by just doing a good job of selling the total value and the benefit of your offering to the lower level contact.

Just as the Brazilian Jiu-Jitsu great Mario Sperry says, "Moves are all *connected*". Many of the strategies, techniques and ideas mentioned earlier are used again in many stages of the **Strategic Selling Cycle**.

Let's remember some earlier points about selling to top executives:

- When given a chance to meet a CXO level prospect, you cannot always approach them the same way as you do lower level contacts.
- Doing your homework and being prepared is a key to your success.
- Having a sponsor who can give you intelligence about the top executives' likes and dislikes, both business and

personal, is important to your success.

- To increase your leverage, try to bring one of your company's executive level managers in and do a team presentation.
- Make sure you coach your company executive, so you go in as a "team", not as two people on a sales call.
- Determine what each of your roles will be before the meeting.
- Preparation increases your leverage and will increase your odds for a successful sales call.

High level executives usually have less time for you to make your case, so be concise. Telling a short "success story" about another customer who you have successfully helped with similar problems is a great way to start off on the right foot. It will show that you are familiar with and have expertise for dealing with the high-level executive's challenges. Think like a consultant, high-level executives want business partners who can help them and their company with their problems and to be more competitive. All this will demonstrate that you have done your homework, but always probe and question deeper into the top level manager's personal perspectives on the problems and challenges of his company's business. Your success will probably be determined by the executive's personal view of success.

Meeting with a high level executive outside of business, such as golfing, at a charity event or sports event, etc. is another great place to close business. Keep it light, but if they should give "buying signals", ask specific questions on how you can help them out. This is an excellent opportunity to close a deal. Better yet, having a prospect's executive and one of your company's high level executives at one of these events is the optimal closing opportunity. Of course, this chance succeeds only if your company's executive takes advantage of an opportunity, should one arise. All CXOs and company executives need to remember my saying, "Everyone is in sales!"

Big Opportunities

Sometimes, when a *sales professional* discovers a big opportunity, he should take the time to stop, take a deep breath and determine a strategic, step-by-step *approach* for winning the business. Winging it, is the best way to guarantee failure. You have to do a thorough job in the **Qualifying stage** for any big opportunity. This is an example of where the stages overlap and you might need to re-qualify the opportunity. You may discover that this is a customer that you and your company can not afford to close. Many questions have to be answered along the way, before the final close.

- Is your company set up now to fulfill and support this prospect or customer?
- Is your company and sales manager committed to fulfillment and support of this prospect's needs?
- Will this prospect be a profitable customer?

You will notice that I didn't ask, "Is the customer committed?" but is your company committed. I have closed many large deals when my company claimed to be committed but quickly forgot after the sale was closed. This left me as a *sales professional*, treading water by myself.

> **KEY TAKEAWAY**
>
> **Sales professionals have to get a sign-off or "buy-in" and commitment from their own top management before moving forward when closing any large deal.**

When I worked for Kinko's, as mentioned previously acquired by FedEx, I closed numerous large deals. On one of the large opportunities, my sales manager helped me write up a one-page overview of the situation. It laid out the details of the *program* and it presented recurring orders, total material needed, timelines, cost and profit. It was a scope letter for the upper operations management of Kinko's. I needed their buy-in and commitment, because this was a big opportunity and it was going to take a large amount of our resources to accomplish. I was selling the deal to my *internal customers*, which happened to be my management. I made them sign off on the deal.

I have produced numerous scope letters for my own company over my sales career. When I worked at Simplex, I made up scope letters and layout drawings for every opportunity I pursued. Then, I had either the project manager or the branch manager review and sign off on every opportunity I sold. As a result, I was probably their most thorough *sales professional*, because I always acquired a buy-in and signed paperwork from my internal management.

Not following through on their commitment to the customer

and the *sales professional* is a mistake many companies make. Unfortunately, I learned the hard way that many companies will not take full responsibly of the **Fulfillment & Support stages** after closing a large deal.

No matter the size of the company, large deals have to be analyzed by others in the company and the *sales professionals*. A little more time must be taken to see if it is a good deal for the customer and the company. The bigger the deal, the bigger the mistakes can be.

Big deals sometimes take the company out of its comfort zone. Most *sales professionals* and companies get excited about big opportunities. That is OK but it is time to slow down and think things through carefully.

> **BIG MISTAKE**
>
> **Wading in too fast for a big opportunity. You could be wading in way over your head.**

Sales professionals need to understand that large deals are opportunities that take extra help to *increase your odds* of closing. *Sales professionals* are usually very proud and independent people, but they need to think of the final part of the sale as a team effort. The team approach is the best way to have *synergy*. The whole is greater than the sum of the individuals' capabilities. Putting all your brains together and working for the common goal will always "increase the odds" of closing the sale.

Controlling the Next Steps & Follow Up

As discussed in the **Prospecting stage**, keeping and controlling *forward momentum* with *next steps* and great *follow up* is one of the top fundamentals to a *sales professional's* success!

Controlling the *next steps* in the buying and closing process is critical to a successful close of any sale. You need to understand the customer's process. Then, if needed, map out the *next steps* to be compatible with your customer's buying process for a successful close.

In an MMA competition, you want to stay in control of the match. When your opponent is in total control or nobody is in control, the chances of victory are substantially reduced.

In sales, the first step is to be in control of the *next steps* that you "can" control. There are many things that you can control regarding *next steps*, all of which can *increase your odds* of a successful close. Try to work together with the customer on both the customer's and your *next steps*. Having sloppy *follow up*, without considering *next steps*, is where many *sales professionals* "drop the ball". If you uncover a need that you can help the potential customer's company with, don't get a *yellow card* for inaction, as in Japanese MMA competitions. When an opportunity has been identified, that is the worst time for no activity or stalling. **A company's number one problem today may not be even a top concern the following month.** Wow! Keep the *forward momentum* going when you uncover an opportunity.

The end of any appointment is always a good time to review what each participant has agreed to do. These are *next steps*. Then ask, "Anything else?" This is a great way to find out something you missed.

When trying to keep your opportunity on track with a potential customer in the **Closing stage**, do not let you or your customer get any *yellow cards*. This means you have to keep things moving. If they are stalling, it can cause both of you to get a y*ellow card*. Remember, getting *yellow cards* in Pride MMA competitions can lead to disqualification. In the sales world, it might only take one to lose the sale. The *sales professional* can lose by not closing the deal and the customer can lose by not benefiting from your company's services. It is the *sales professional's* ultimate responsibility to try to keep the action going and keep control over the *next steps*.

KEY TAKEAWAY
Do not let you or your customers get any "yellow cards" because of stalling or inactivity.

Closing B2B – business-to-business deals almost always require a series of steps leading to the close. There are numerous examples of being in charge of making the *next steps*:

- Scheduling your next *follow up* meeting at the end of your first appointment.
- Getting cost estimates for the prospect in a timely manner.
- Calling them back after they return to town in two months.
- Recommend scheduling a site visit for the next step with

a time and date.

- Schedule calling back in six months to see if anything has changed.
- Asking the customer what the *next steps* should be.

It is imperative that you always schedule any and all *follow up* meetings, including your next appointment. Reponses to customer requests should be scheduled, as well as how you are going to get that information back to them. Even if they tell you the next scheduled meeting will have to be tentative, that is OK. It is much easier for you to reschedule your next meeting than to schedule the next one down the line, when the urgency has subsided. This is one of your first opportunities to impress the potential customer. If possible, include another letter of recommendation with a note, "Here is another pleased customer whose bottom line we helped improve. They had challenges similar to the ones you are facing."

After a while, the *next steps* will become very systemized. If I had a great meeting with a potential customer and they told me that things look promising for a partnership, I always sent them a quick follow up thanking them for the meeting, mentioning that I was looking forward to meeting them again on (insert date and time) and that I looked forward to getting the opportunity to work together.

A different kind of next step might be to note in your CRM system that this customer should be abandoned. Yes, this is a perfectly acceptable next step if there just isn't a fit. I note the date I abandoned the prospect. It is amazing how my fellow *sales professionals* or I will come back across the same prospect a year later, discovering that their situation has changed and now they are a prospect again. The key is that I have some *intelligence* in my CRM system and it provides a head start the second time around. This is just another reason for why it is crucial to fully utilize a CRM system in today's business environment.

Laying out your *next steps* or always trying to have a *next step* in mind is a key to helping to *increase your odds* of closing a sale. Just as in the **Prospecting Strategy stage**, when closing, the *sales professional* has to keep the action moving forward, no *yellow cards* for you or the customer. If you leave the *forward momentum* totally up to the customer, this could lead to a *yellow card* and change the opportunity to a "no decision". A high percentage of deals are lost, not to competition, but to no decisions by the customers. Many would say that the prospect wasn't adequately qualified. This might be the case, but there are just as many instances where the *sales professional* has allowed the customer to get several *yellow cards*. The urgency fades, the customer stalls and finally the *forward momentum* stops.

It is the *sales professional's* main responsibility to keep the *forward momentum* going. Remember, "Keeping the ball in your court" helps you keep the process moving forward. Examples can be: writing up the scope letter with start dates and getting the customer to sign and commit to the dates. This will remind the customer that you need their approval to meet the all important delivery date, so that you can get the resources together to make it happen for them. If a customer is really busy, you need to keep attempting to control the process. Tell them that you will call them the following Monday to get the final approval, after they have had their meeting. Especially in today's ultra-competitive and ultra-fast paced world, **YOU MUST** keep the customer on track. Much of this necessary attention to detail can be automated in your CRM system.

I have had instances where I have gotten verbal approval, "Going with you and your company is the right thing for our company", I have heard variations of this type of verbal approval and I have learned the hard way that it isn't over until it is over. Even if you have done a great job of selling the value of your company's products and services and the contact is sold, it doesn't take long for the urgency to wear off. Other pressing issues can creep up and steal the attention away from you and your solutions.

Trying to finish a fight in the MMA competition is all about *forward momentum.* You can launch body forward with a strike or takedown. The same goes in the **Closing stage**; it is all about keeping things moving forward. Yes, you will have setbacks, but *sales professionals* have to keep momentum going forward all the way to the close. Many *sales professionals* wonder why they lost a deal that seemed so completely sold only to have the customer stop returning their calls. Then, it ends up in one of the studies as a no decision, with the *sales professional* still wondering what happened. Many times it is because they let the customer get several *yellow cards*, causing the *sales professional* to get disqualified and lose their commission.

On a very big *project* for one of Kinko's largest customers, I uncovered a desperate need with tight deadlines for our products and services. I told the customer contact I was willing to commit my company's resources to meet their deadlines but that a written commitment was needed first before final approval. I found out that my contact needed the signature of his boss's boss. Next, I told my contact that I needed him to help schedule a meeting with that other person in the next two days. I told him I would make my calendar as open as possible so we could help him look good. As illustrated, this decision to proceed initiated a series of *next steps*.

Think of the *next steps* like playing chess, where you must always think of your *next steps* in advance.

Last Ditch Effort

Sometimes, I have made a last attempt to close a customer. Many times I was unsuccessful. However, if you have invested any time at all, you owe it to yourself to try one last time. Be sure you do not burn your bridges, however. Here is where some sales experts may disagree with me. Remember that there are many *Truths* and one thing that has worked for me is to just come out and finally ask, "What will it take to get a chance to prove myself?" or "What will it take to get a piece of your business?" At such a moment, I have had a customer reply that in a month or so they would give me a chance. Just being forward, trying not to be too pushy but pleasantly persistent, has helped me acquire some business that otherwise would have been lost.

If nothing else, it gets me a commitment from the customer that I can call them back in three to six months to see if there are any opportunities. I have usually invested a certain amount of time at this point, so it doesn't take much effort to give them a call back to see if there are any opportunities or maybe even a *change in guard*.

Winning the Business... Now What to Do?

When you close the sale, the first thing you need to do is thank the new customer for giving you and your company an opportunity to help them out. Then you need to do what you said you would do. "Make it easy to do business" with your company. This is where I have learned that you can start off the relationship on a good tone right out of the gate. Does the new customer have to be set up with your company before the fulfillment of the first order? There are often some logistics that have to be worked out. Depending on the type and size of the customer, there can be many different things to be set up. One of the most important first steps for your company is to make it easy for a first time customer to get set up to start buying from your company.

I have worked for many companies where if the *sales professional* didn't *babysit* the initial setup we would have "dropped the ball" with the first order. Companies need to take responsibility for most of the initial set up of a new customer and the fulfillment of the first order. The *sales professional* should not need to oversee the process to ensure that the initial setup is complete.

At my present employer, I try to impress any new customer right out of the gate. In the first 24 to 48 business hours, I coordinate website setup, customer accounts setup and any other logistical issues. Most customers are very impressed and tell me that this type of service is rare. That is exactly what I want them to say. They are indirectly telling my company and me that the previous vendor has done exactly opposite to what we strive to do, under promise and over perform.

Now is a perfect time to ask important questions: "What was the main reason you choose our company?", "What did you like and what would you have changed about the previous vendor?" I have found that the customer very often opens up after they have committed to your company. The *intelligence* gained here and now can be some of the best about your competitors' strengths and weaknesses. You will find there are some patterns that start to develop in certain types of business, and then you can make sure you stress that important aspect every time you are trying to close that particular type of business. Again, this type of questioning, after you have won the business, is invaluable for winning new business in the future.

Getting Tapped Out/Learning from Losing

Every time an opponent gives me trouble while competing, such as when I am grappling with some of the people that I train with and one of them "taps me out", I get caught in a choke or arm or leg lock and I submit, lose the match. However, I always try to learn from that defeat. I will think about what I could have done differently, what mistakes I made and, most importantly, how can I avoid it happening again.

I will even talk about it with my training partners and ask for their input. This type of constant self-evaluation helps me continually to improve my technique. I also can learn from others' mistakes when they get tapped out.

The same approach should be followed in the sales world; sales managers and *sales professionals* need to learn from their losses. Take time to analyze any mistakes. Could you have done anything differently? Was this deal never in the cards? Did someone drop the ball? Did you let the customer drop the ball? You need to analyze and learn from your losses. This will certainly help increase the odds in all future sales opportunities.

In the sales world, we are always going to "get tapped out" sooner or later, but we have to use our mistakes and losses to make future sales. Gerhard Gschwandtner, publisher of Selling Power, said it best and is one of the next key takeaways.

KEY TAKEAWAY

"Turn all your setbacks into comebacks."

Gerhard Gschwandtner, Personal Selling Power

As in all stages of the **Strategic Selling Cycle**, closing is a constant learning endeavor. You always try to properly prepare your *setup/approach*, utilizing all of your *leverage*. This will lead to "increasing your odds" of closing the sale and opening a long-term, profitable relationship with your new customer.

Objections and rejections are probably the top reasons why *sales professionals* are hesitant to prospect and close more deals. It is human nature to avoid rejection, but only people who can handle rejection and keep plugging should seek a profession in sales. Accordingly, it is always my goal to reduce both my objections and rejections. Although as a *sales professional*, I might be able to take it better than persons not in sales, I still don't enjoy facing a loss or defeat. It is just human nature, but this aversion to getting beaten in either the martial arts or sales drives me constantly to become better at what I do, and that is the competitive and fun part of both endeavors.

KEY TAKEAWAY

"The only difference between those who succeed and those who don't is that successful people act in spite of their fear, doubt and worry. So can you!"

Jeffrey Gitomer, top sales author and sales expert

7

Fulfillment & Support Strategy Stages

Fulfillment & Support are where the wheels fall off
the sales process in most companies.

The easiest part of most Sales Professionals' job is
selling; it is the rest that is the hard part.

This chapter on the next two stages of the **Strategic Selling Cycle**, Fulfillment and Support blur together at many companies. However, more than ever, they have to be studied separately to better understand them, and ultimately, each will be one of the keys to happy customers and a successful sales force.

For what will be covered in this chapter, I wish I could just put what I have heard several young teenagers say, "Well duh!"

I am going to make a bold statement: If companies truly would handle the **Fulfillment & Support Strategy stages** properly, sales could double. These two stages are the most non-revenue-generating activities of the **Strategic Selling Cycle** for a sales force, but they are the ones that "suck" up a lot of the *sales professionals'* time.

It would appear to be common sense for most companies to understand the importance and the severity of the problem that fulfillment and support need to be the main responsibilities of the company, not their sales force. The following are some *Truths* and *Universal Truths* that I have discovered while working in seven different industries over 20 years in sales. Again, studies back up my personal experience and observations.

> **BIG MISTAKE**
>
> **When the easiest part of selling is closing the new business. The toughest part is getting one's own company to provide what they have promised.**

In the **Closing Strategy stage**, I gave an example that, at times, coming up with an accurate price was a huge task, and I related the story of how it took *sales professionals* more time to come up with pricing than the time spent with the customer on a sales call. What a big but very common mistake!

Submitting accurate orders has become easier but still has a long way to go. Still, submitting orders can lower the performance of the sales force overall. Therefore, companies need a large study to figure out what should be common sense: submitting orders should not be more difficult than getting an order.

> **KEY TAKEAWAY**
>
> **Submitting orders shouldn't be tougher than getting orders.**

My adage that the toughest part of my job isn't closing new business but to rely on my company to provide what we have *promised* was presented in the **Closing Strategy stage**. This issue remains a problem for many *sales professionals* and continues to be a major failing of many companies.

Some studies have shown repeatedly that *sales professionals* only spend 20-30 percent of their time interacting with potential and current customers. That leaves 70-80 percent of the sales force's time doing other non-revenue-generating activities. Wow! What a waste of sales talent.

What are the *sales professionals* doing? Are they out messing around, playing golf or taking off early? The low performer may be; but, I believe that most of this time the reliable and talented *sales professionals* are acting as the fulfillment and support departments, along with doing administrative activities, e.g., sales reports and paperwork.

What is the answer most companies come up with to solve this problem? Many of the *sales professionals* I interviewed over the last few years have told me that their companies did the same things as the ones I have worked for. The companies' managements became very adamant that the *sales professionals* were supposed to be out of the office making calls from 8:00am to 4:00pm every day. So, what were the fulfillment and support departments doing to bolster those sales efforts?

KEY TAKEAWAY
Common sense isn't always common practice.

"Can you handle the truth?" I feel most companies are ready to handle the truth, because the environment is just too competitive and they are looking for real answers to many of the age-old problems of sales forces not meeting their goals. If companies truly want their sales force to sell, then they have to commit to successfully handling the **Fulfillment & Support stages**.

What is Fulfillment?

It is keeping a promise for whatever has been agreed upon: products, service or both; to make or provide something to that customer for a particular cost. It is to satisfy your *promise* to the customer, the making, producing and/or delivering of a product or service. Once a *sales professional* closes a new deal, whether it is new business or more business, how the company sustains the *promise* made in the sales agreement determines whether the *sales professional* feels safe in beginning the hunt for more business.

Support is supposed to occur after the product is delivered. This seems straightforward, but it is not for many companies.

When I worked for Warner Lambert, I would sell a certain quantity of promotional displays for a certain product, such as Sinutab. The implied *promise* was certain promotional displays, a specific quantity, SKU's (stock keeping units), a barcoded number, prices and specific deliver dates. If there was a problem, I never knew about it. I never had to worry about any of the fulfillment; it was completely taken care of by my company.

Companies need to take responsibility for the success or failure of their sales forces. A coach on a football team gets the credit or blame for how well a team does during the season. It is the coach's job to get rid of any football player not pulling his weight. If the team does badly the coach gets the blame, right or wrong; but if the owner, i.e., the company, does not support the coach with money and resources to recruit and train the best, the coach is limited.

In the sales world, I read sales consultant after sales expert saying it is up to the *sales professional* to quit making excuses, "You are the only one who controls your success" or "Nobody else is stopping you from being successful but you." Many of these sales consultants/ experts will tell stories of how once the *sales professionals* quit making excuses, the major obstacles to their success are removed. Some sales consultants/experts even go on to say that once the *sales professionals* stop whining, sales will miraculously skyrocket.

I do agree that even in a bad company, with a bad sales manager, *sales professionals* can still be successful. A great attitude is a key but not *The Truth* to successful sales. Many companies have their heads in the sand regarding the fact that they cause the biggest obstacles to their sale forces. Companies, like a football team's owners and coaches, have to take the lead in responsibility of a sales force's success or failure.

> **BIG MISTAKE**
> **Most sales forces' biggest obstacles are caused by their own company.**

Back to the studies that find that *sales professionals* only spend 20-30 percent of their time interacting with customers. I am willing to bet that if a company would actually commit to handling fulfillment and support, the time would double to at least 40-60 percent of salespeople's time being spent interacting with customers. Just think of how many more successful *sales professionals* and sales forces such companies could have. Once a company truly takes total responsibility for the **Fulfillment stage**, then and only then should companies worry about chronic whining from their *sales professionals*.

Companies tend to blame their sales forces for underachievement, but maybe companies should look in the collective mirror and ask, "Are we truly supporting our sales force? Are we doing a good job with the **Fulfillment & Support stages** of the **SSC**?" Ask yourself, "Can I handle the truth?"

At Kinko's, I would *promise* to sell the customer a certain quantity of human resource binders with a specific number of pages, ink types, binding and delivery dates.

At ITG, Intermountain Technology Group, things were more complicated on the *promise*, i.e., a scope letter was needed that included specific details of the upgrade to an existing networks operating system and installation of new hardware. There were many details including new software, new hardware, ITG technician labor, a price point, milestone dates and a final completion date.

Once a *sales professional* gets an order, she needs to ask herself what are the steps, *next steps*, and the order of operations to meet the needed date for the final delivery of the product or service. Who is going to be responsible for each step? Most important, who is going to be accountable for each step? Many companies get confused and don't do a good job of holding operations accountable for the delivery of the *promise*, so, the *sales professional* has to get involved to different degrees, both mentally and physically, to help ensure the *promise* is fulfilled.

As mentioned before, when I worked at Simplex, I also did scope letters and layout drawings that were signed off before the close by the manager or project manager on every potential job that I was trying to sell. I was probably the most thorough at making sure I always had buy-off and signed paperwork from my management.

I produced internal scope letters to help educate the company on the size and scope of the projected business I had the opportunity to bring in, but unfortunately, I did it mainly as a tool "to hold them accountable" for what we had *promised* to the customer.

I learned the hard way that companies are eager to get the big deals but are quick to forget the promises and commitments they have made.

Turning in an Order - This is Where the Wheels Fall Off

The *sales professional* has worked hard, done his job and brought in some new business. All the *sales professional* has to do is drop off the order and go back out to close some more business, right? I have found that such a question can only be answered in the affirmative in a fantasy world. From my experience, the *sales professional* ends up being a *babysitter* for much of the business they bring in, at least if they want their orders to be completed as *promised*.

Example: An MMA competitor has trained for months for a big fight. At the end of round two, he gets cut above his right eye. Such cuts can lead to stopping the fight if the bleeding continues. The bell rings and he goes to his corner. "Where is the stool? It was there at the end of the first round", he says. "Oh, the corner man had to leave early." As the fighter leans against the cage, he asks, "Where is my cut man?" "Oh, he is new. Can you help him with how to stop a cut that bad?" "The water bottle is empty?" "Oh, your other corner guy forgot to fill it up, he will have it for you the next round, hopefully." Not being able to rest adequately, the lack of water and the bleeding from the cut could contribute to the fighter losing the fight.

Does this sound far-fetched? If you did a large survey of *sales professionals*, I bet you 90+ percent would laugh, because this story will ring true and this situation will not be far from what goes on in their company.

The fighter is trained to be a fighter, not a cut man, not a trainer for a cut man and not a corner man. He is a fighter, and his main job is to win fights.

Now, you have a *sales professional* out in the field, the "Sales Cage", and the *sales professional* continually gets calls, "Where is the order I placed?" "I need to make a change to my last order", "The pricing is wrong on my last invoice; it is not what we agreed to." Or the *sales professional* stops by his office and someone has left him an email that XYZ Company is not happy because their order arrived late and they want the *sales professional* to call them immediately. Here is another disturbing scenario: ABC Company, your biggest account, can't seem to get anyone in Customer Service to return their calls. Does the next one sound familiar? The *sales professional's* last order is sitting on her desk with a note that someone from the operations department has some questions before they will start the project. However, there was a detailed scope letter signed by the operations manager that explained everything

As covered in the **Closing Strategy Stage**, when I worked for ITG - Intermountain Technology Group, I would take my customers through a discovery session and then have my subject experts come up with a scope letter. Now the deal has been closed. The *next steps* are experiences that, unfortunately, I have been a part of. This is where the "Wheels Fall Off".

I always explained to all my customers that my job was to understand their challenges and problems and to bring in the resources needed to solve their problems. Many *sales professionals* try to be the resource "know it all" and that is a BIG MISTAKE. Then, every time there is a problem in the middle of the Fulfillment or Support of the project, they will be calling their *sales professional*. A sales person's main task is to focus on gaining trust and closing the deal, not having to be a *babysitter*.

What is needed is to educate the customer on the key contacts in the company who have the knowledge of the project and can help them if any issues come up. This approach will allow the *sales professional* to go out and get some more sales. A sales person can check in with the customer to make sure everything is going as planned. Remember, if you are a *sales professional* or an account manager, you are managing the sales to the customers; you are not the main person "Fulfilling and Supporting" what you have sold. Others in the company have to be responsible and accountable for the Fulfillment and the Support to the customers.

Some small companies will disagree with this line of thinking, but it is a *Truth*, if not a *Universal Truth*.

KEY TAKEAWAY

Sales Professionals need to be selling and not be the Fulfillment & Support departments for the company.

I have heard many times, "You are a sales consultant, sales representative, corporate account manager, etc., but you are not an order taker. Sales get paid too much to be just that." Well, I guess with that same logic, I am NOT a data entry person, hotline for customer service or for shipping or for operations or manufacturing. Also, I am not an administrative assistant for sales, etc.

Gerhard Gschwandtner, publisher of *Selling Power* magazine, has interviewed hundreds of companies' sales executives in almost every industry imaginable. He is quoted as saying, "You don't want to turn your *sales professionals* into data entry people." However, at one of my companies, that is exactly what they did. S*ales professionals* were trained on our new system to enter their own orders and to become the data entry department. At this company, the orders were normally very complex; were composed of many parts, with many different part numbers; and pricing was very complex. I ended up "bribing" one of the few customer service people left, who had done data entry for years, by giving her sandwiches. She entered my orders, so I could spend more time in the field, knowing that my orders would be correct. Many of the orders entered by the *sales professionals* were incorrectly put in and this caused a lot of change orders to be done.

> **BIG MISTAKE**
> **When a sales forces' biggest obstacle to success in sales is their own company.**

One of our main competitors in the collections industry, who is many times larger than both our companies combined, was the subject of inside *intelligence* that one of their strategic goals was to put us out of business. They have many resources and competition is fierce. Many of their tactics, I would say, bordered on the unethical side.

Luckily, the owner of my company agrees with my thinking and my MSA methodology. My biggest obstacle in the past, my own company, actually is helping me to succeed now. They are truly doing a great job on the **Fulfillment & Support stages**, which frees up more of my time to focus on sales and the **SSC**. As a result, our company has been very successful the last five years and has broken many records regarding profit and new business. By helping me stay out of the **Fulfillment & Support stages** a majority of the time and letting me focus on the **Retention**, **Qualifying**, **Prospecting**, **Closing** and **Expanding Strategy stages**, I have been able to be very successful. My boss has allowed me to spend a majority of my time in the *revenue-generating* stages of the **SSC**.

What is Support?

Usually, once a product or service is sold; there is some type of support of that product or service. Companies can support their products and services by maintaining, reinforcing and strengthening them. Again, this should not be the main responsibility of the sales force or a *sales professional.*

However companies choose to define **Fulfillment & Support** on the **SSC**, they need to be able to support the **SSC** stages to the fullest.

The **Support stage** mainly comes into play after the product or service has been delivered, but it can begin as soon as the purchase order has been signed and invoicing and shipping has started.

There are crossovers, such as in the middle of a project: Where are the rest of my parts? The invoicing is wrong? Where is my order? This is where many companies just don't have clear policies, procedures and processes in place to handle all the support needs of their customers.

Again, support is not a *revenue-generating activity* most of the time. It can be if the customer needs one more widget, but should they have to call the *sales professional* for one more widget? Of course not, because there should be a support structure in place. If support is billable, as at ITG or when calling for extra help from Simplex technicians, then that is even more of a reason not to have *sales professionals* giving away expertise for free.

Experts referring to the **Support stage** have said that *Sales Professional*s should give customers their cellular phone number and be available after hours. I disagree, although there may be an exception for something like a one-person sales company, most B2B – business-to-business companies need to have a reliable support structure in place, not your *sales professional* answering questions at their dinner table. This goes back to my original premise: companies that want their *sales professionals* to be the most successful have to "be" the **fulfillment** and **support** for their customers, not their sales force. Your sales force should not be the backup for customer support, yet if you did a large survey of *sales professionals,* I believe that most would respond that they are many times the backup to the customer support hotline. BIG MISTAKE!

> **BIG MISTAKE**
> **When your sales force "is" the backup for the company's weak customer support hotline.**

One of my favorite sales experts, coaches and trainers agrees with me. Dave Kahle said, "It is kind of inherent for sales to bend over backwards for their customers, at every customer's whim." Just as I have learned and stated, you have to train your customers to use others inside the company for fulfillment and support. As we have discussed before, this will let the *sales professional* focus more of his or her time on sales.

I was listening to Audio-Tech Business book reviews for *Slack: Getting Past Burnout, Busywork, and the Myth of Total Efficiency,* by Tom Demarco. His research reinforces that my thinking has been correct when he states that much of clerical work has been reduced and eliminated because of automation, but that some of the administrative support work has been pushed up to middle management, to sales and even higher. Remember my example of the company that I worked for laying off part of their data entry personnel and training the sales force to do their own order entry? What a BIG MISTAKE!

I had the privilege to talk to a high-level government official. This person would be considered a CXO level in the private sector. He told me that much of the support structure had been removed and that through automation he was supposed to do what had previously been the responsibility of a support person. It now took him many hours per week to be an administrative support for his own position. I think that if someone did the numbers they would find that the true cost, his time plus the opportunity cost, would more than pay for additional hours to be worked by an administrative support person.

The recent studies and books on this subject have stated what I have known for years. Many companies have gone too far by thinking that automation will eliminate the need for many support people, pushing the administrative tasks up and out, out to the outside *sales professionals*. The trend upward might be relatively new but it has been happening to sale forces for years

Bill McDermott, CEO and President of SAP America Inc. used a great analogy that sums up this issue nicely.

KEY TAKEAWAY

"The *sales professional* might be the quarterback, but he needs other people to run the plays."

Bill McDermott, SAP CEO and President

Landing the Big One and Trying to Support It

One of my fellow *sales professionals* in an earlier company uncovered a huge opportunity. She secured the business of a new customer and began many *programs* with them. Remember, *programs* should be the goal. This is business that keeps on going; the customer has to keep reordering, refilling, etc.

This new customer was caught up in the dot com boom. Their growth was straight up, as with many companies during that era.

My fellow *sales professional* and I used to disagree on the role of Fulfillment and Support. She felt that I needed to be more understanding that many of our co-workers weren't paid very well and we couldn't expect too much from them. In my very biased opinion, this is an excuse for not making people responsible and accountable for their jobs.

This customer's purchases became so large that the *sales professional* spent all of her time helping with the **Fulfillment & Support stages**. She "was" the manager of this customer's fulfillment and support. She was the full time *babysitter* of this client. I don't mean any disrespect to her personally; it is just that her attentiveness to her client's needs reinforced that the success or failure of our business with this customer was in her hands. I do have to give her credit, because she did an outstanding job. However, her customer became more and more demanding of our company's resources and all of her sales time. She made up many reference and training manuals for co-workers to help them be able to Fulfill and Support the customer better. This ate up any extra selling time she might have had available.

She was the "Sales Person of the Year" for our company, which was a great honor. We had over 500 *sales professionals* across the United States. Her branch won numerous awards. She made a great deal of money and so did her branch. Certainly, our company made a nice profit from this business.

Next, my co-worker won a trip to go along with her award. Unfortunately, during the same time period, her big customer started to have financial problems, reducing orders and becoming ever more demanding of the branch's and her time.

Then, it happened. The big customer filed for bankruptcy, as many did towards the end of the dot com era.

Now, what became of the *sales professional?* Ninety percent of her monthly quota was covered by sales to this former big customer. The branch's and her quotas are both sky high, and it took a year for their numbers to be adjusted down. The *sales professional* went from a yearly income of six figures to $30,000 per year and was expected to build her territory back up.

Did the company feel a responsibility to the *sales professional?* She made the branch manager and the company a lot of money over several years. Actually, our top management did what most companies I have worked for have done, nothing. They felt this huge loss of business was the *sales professional's* problem.

Should she have been out in the field more looking for new business to diversify her customer base? Surely, but the company should have been doing its job with **Fulfillment & Support stages** for this big customer. Or they should have made a decision that the *sales* *professional* was making a sacrifice. Then, they should have worked with her if that huge piece of business went away.

I have seen this scenario occur time and time again at companies I have worked for. The *sales professional* becomes a full time account manager for the one big client. The one main recurring problem is that without the *babysitting* by the *sales professional*, most companies have a hard time keeping big customers. This volume of business can be very demanding of everyone's time and resources. Most *sales professionals* would not turn down the opportunity to land the big fish. The prestige, recognition and money are almost irresistible.

Companies, managers and *sales professionals* have to think about the **Fulfillment & Strategy stages** and how they are going to handle and support each stage. This is especially important for large customers. How are they going to support the *sales professional* before and after the sale? That is the critical question that needs to be addressed and answered.

Sell It and We Will Support It?

Many companies want their sales forces to bring in any and all business; the more the better. When I worked for Simplex, Service Division, I communicated my concern that I was selling more than we could support. The branch manager told me, "You sell it and I will just hire more people if we need more support." Unfortunately, by the time the new co-workers were hired, trained and in the field for support, I had sold even more. We were always behind and much of my time was spent *babysitting* and acting as backup for our overwhelmed customer support people. As mentioned before, our branch was number one in the United States the two years I was the branch's only *sales professional*. Imagine how much more business I or any good *sales professional* could have brought in if I were not also the backup for Customer Support.

When I worked for Kinko's, there was a big opportunity. None of the other *sales professionals* really wanted this particular customer, because they had an in-house print shop. Everyone had forgotten that our area's largest customer also had a print shop.

My strategy was to become their first choice for overflow. I wanted us to be the backup for *projects* or *programs* that their in-house print shop needed help to fulfill. It took some work, but I finally convinced the customer contact, we will call her Nancy, to give me an *order starter*, a small order to prove myself. The order was for about $180. I worked hard to make sure that the order was delivered on time. What I didn't do was *babysit* the **Fulfillment stage**. The customer called and left a message that the job was very messed up. In such a situation, I try to do a little background check to see if the paperwork gave any clues as to what happened. The paperwork looked in order; final quality check was signed off. Then, I called the customer back as quickly as possible; putting the call off will many times just let the customer get more aggravated.

The customer said the job looked very unprofessional. She should have known because she had run a very large print shop for years. I used the technique that has been successful for years, "I am sorry, we are sorry, no excuses, we dropped the ball, but I will do whatever it takes to make things right". Usually this starts to cool the customer down. I apologized; I admitted that I made a mistake, and asked what it would take to fix it. I didn't avoid the problem; I addressed it head on.

Usually the customers will ask for a discount, less than I would have been willing to give them. This time was the first time the customer asked for a total refund. This request caught me off guard, but I had talked to the branch manager before I called and she left it, the decision, up to me. I told the customer that it was fine, if that is what it would take, along with my apologies again.

The branch manager wasn't happy with my giving a total refund. The thing she missed was that the job was totally messed up, pages in wrong order, copies crooked and dumped in the boxes. I went to the site and picked up the order to be re-run. It was badly done and I was embarrassed. I apologized again and told Nancy that things will go wrong sometimes. I apologized again and said it was so soon in our relationship but that I would always be there to make things right. Then, I went back to make sure the order was run properly and I personally delivered it back the same day. She seemed impressed but still not too friendly and I couldn't blame her.

I tell this story from my past as an illustration of how companies repeatedly will not take responsibility and accountability for supporting their customers and their sales force.

Did I blow my only chance with this large customer who no one else wanted? No. Nancy called me the next month with a ten thousand dollar order, without bidding. She just gave it to me. She started ordering from me on an on-going basis, and I was her first backup whenever their in-house print shop couldn't make a deadline. After

I left Kinko's, I was told she stopped using their services, and in this case, the reason she was buying again was because of her relationship with me.

I ran into Nancy years later while having lunch and I told her that I was going to put her story in my book. I also told her I always liked dealing with her, because she was a straight shooter, no games; just do what you say you will do. She thanked me and told me she enjoyed working with me but that some people didn't like her style, because it was too straightforward. Wow, who wouldn't want a customer who didn't play games, and just expected you to provide the products and services as you had promised? I found it easy to keep our promises, but many companies do not. They tend to make excuses for not providing what was *promised*.

As with a MMA fighter or any top up-and-coming fighter, some support is required. They usually have sponsors to bring in some money and cover part of their expenses so they do not have to worry too much about expenditures. Then, they can simply focus both mentally and physically on their training and their next fight.

Money concerns can severely distract a fighter from his training. Physically, it can cause a distraction because the fighter will need another job, which disrupts a training routine.

Similarly, the *sales professional* can be distracted from prospecting with mental distractions: will the company correctly handle the orders he just turned in? There can also be physical distractions: I just turned in another job that I still have to be involved in because the company has poor fulfillment and I have to *babysit* the job through the **Fulfillment stage**.

Companies wishing to be the most successful will need to consider how "they" will support large customers before they acquire such customers. If they choose to move forward, companies have to commit, to be accountable and to support both the customer and *sales professional*. Before and after any big customers sign the dotted line, it is a good idea to try to meet in the middle. Don't encourage your sales force to bring in all the business they can without the company's committing to being on the same team.

Co-workers Who Don't Care

Sales professionals will just laugh about how typical this next part rings true, but for companies and top management, again, "Can you handle the truth?"

It has happened to me time and time again that co-workers seriously upset a customer. Many co-workers just do not have the same attitude as *sales professionals.* Some have a poor attitude and do not care about the customer's needs or success.

When I came back to one of the companies that I worked for twice, there was a list of customer names on the wall with *projects* and *programs* due dates listed next to each. Many of the names I recognized and I mentioned one customer, who had grown very demanding, to a co-worker. He then said, "She is a cow most of the time", and I was caught off guard. Then, I mentioned another on-going customer that I had started up with when I previously worked there and the co-worker said he could be a real jerk.

Sales professionals might look at those same two customers and say, "Those two are my top customers and they expect top of the line service". Then I remembered that negative attitudes were prevalent with this company's operations workers. When there are bad attitudes in Operations, the people sales forces rely on to provide what has been *promised,* it will have a huge impact on the sales force, which is expected to be the *revenue-generating* machine. Such bad attitudes end up making the sales force feel they have to *babysit* their jobs, which takes away time both mentally and physically that should be focused on bringing in more sales!

Poor attitudes often come from management, sometimes from top management. I have talked to numerous *sales professionals* who tell me that you just have to learn to live with these types of negative feelings. Many times, top management comes to visit and I have noticed all the co-workers "acting" very friendly and pretending that they care, until the top managers leave. Then, it is back to the same old negative environment.

I use a saying for this situation. It is from the movie *The Wizard of Oz,* "Pay no attention to the man behind the curtain." Maybe the top managers do want to know the truth. There is a very common problem at many of the companies I have worked for and seems to be common with other *sales professionals* who I have interviewed and talked with. Many companies have problems that are being concealed from top management. Worse yet, many times *sales professionals* are trying not to let their customers "look behind the curtain". If they did, they would find out that the *sales professionals* are in the minority when it comes to caring about the customer's success.

> **BIG MISTAKE**
>
> **When Sale Professionals have to tell their customers "Don't look behind the curtain."**

Sales Professionals Create More Work for Co-workers

The fact that *sales professionals* create work for others in the company seems to be obvious, but the fact that top management "lets" that new work affect the attitudes is totally unacceptable.

Numerous *sales professionals* have told me that they have experienced the same situation. When bringing in new business, especially a large new *project* or *program*, they can expect moaning and groaning from many co-workers. *Sales professionals* create more work for their co-workers. Even if a co-worker does not have a negative attitude towards the customers, the fact is that with tight timelines and stream-lined work forces, the pressure and stress is greater than ever before. Now, to compound these challenges with customers becoming more and more demanding because of competition, a *sales professional* bringing in more business is not always greeted well by co-workers. This type of mentality is more common than many companies will admit. Often, companies don't want to know the truth, because they do not want to have to deal with it. The bottom line is that many employees in companies just don't have the same positive, caring attitude regarding customers as management and *sales professionals* do.

What are the Solutions for Great Fulfillment and Support?

Can your company handle the truth? First I will address most companies; they continue to make excuses and not take full responsibility for the fulfillment and support of products and services.

For all that we discuss here, you will have to adjust and tweak it to make it work for you.

Sales professionals have to be "problem solvers" to be top *salespeople*, and problem-solving skills do come in handy to solve your own company's problems and shortfalls in **Fulfillment & Strategy stages**. This is not to say that you should try to solve all your company's problems. What you want to focus on is working around your company's inability or refusal to accept responsibility for Fulfilling and Supporting of their products and services. Here are a few ideas and workarounds I have discovered through problem solving that have helped me spend more time selling and less *babysitting.*

Learning too much about the fulfillment and support process is <u>not</u> always a good idea. Yes, it might make you look smart, but if you will do it for no charge, customers will start relying on you for the Support. When I worked at Kinko's, several times I saw *sales professionals* helping to put together an order, because operations was short of staff that day. Then these *sales professionals* would drop off the order to the customer, because the delivery department was also short of staff. Now these *sales professionals* had become backup personnel for the **Fulfillment & Support stages.** BIG MISTAKE!

I know what some people might be thinking: "Scott is not a team player." On the contrary, I quickly take out the trash and make the coffee, which are small tokens of my appreciation for my co-workers. However, I try not to fall into the trap that many of my fellow *sales professionals* did, becoming "sucked in" to be the backup for **Fulfillment** and **Support stages** when help was needed. Yes, at times I did deliver orders for the branches; but, it was "strategic", a way to drop by to touch base with the customer. The best help a *sales professional* can give to all co-workers is be out selling and bringing in more business that will help every co-worker with job security.

Giving every customer your cellular phone number is a BIG MISTAKE. It is customers' human nature to call you first because it is easy. That is what your company wants, fewer calls for them. However, an unintended consequence is less selling for you and them. Something that has worked very well for me is to set up my office line to page my cellular with any new messages. That way, I can be very responsive to any messages. I also let customers know that I check my emails at the first of the day and at the end of the day, because I am out with other customers the rest of the time. The next step is to train your customers to contact other people. Supply phone numbers and email addresses for your "go to's", co-workers that you have confidence will take care of your customer to the level you expect. Many times, these are the same co-workers mentioned in the **Prospecting Strategy stage** who I took extra care of with small tokens of appreciation, such as sandwiches, cookies, coffee, and freebies from trade shows. They are my top *"internal customers"*. These co-workers can and are keys to your success. They can free up a lot of your time that would have been spent *babysitting* and this will free you up to do more *revenue-generating activities.*

> **BIG MISTAKE**
>
> **Giving every customer your cell phone number will turn you over night into the Customer Support hotline.**

By providing customers with other key contacts in your company on one page, they can put it up on a wall for a quick reference. Your name should not be anywhere on that page. Mention to the customer that you are usually out with other customers, so for the best and quickest support, this sheet lists the key contacts that can assist them 24 hours a day. The names on the sheet are your personal picks; because you have faith in these co-workers' abilities to assist your customers.

Always let your customers know that if there is ever a problem they can't get resolved through these support channels you have provided, then you will help them.

I have done the same thing for years, either a team member or myself, by sending a congratulations letter to all new clients listing our departments and contact information. Companies should put the same information on their websites.

Once I had a sales manager ask me what I was doing differently by working with co-workers. He had been dealing with numerous complaints from other *sales professionals* and they were complaining that many of their projects were being done incorrectly. At the time, I was not aware of what I was doing differently, but now looking back, I can see that I was helping reinforce the support structure for **Fulfillment & Support** through several of my techniques and strategies. One of my main keys was to educate my customers on other reliable contacts for questions and assistance.

> **KEY TAKEAWAY**
>
> **Make it easy to work with you and easy to deal with your company.**

Sales Support

I have had official Sales Support at two companies that I have worked for. The Sales Support was supposed to support the sales force. Looking back, Sales Support was kind of an offshoot of marketing. Not much that they sent out was very useful. If they did do beneficial activities for the sales force, we never were told or knew of those activities.

For there to be beneficial and productive sales support, the sales force needs to be questioned, surveyed on what is useful to the *sales professional* in the field. Has Sales Support ever come along on any sales calls? If not, how can they understand the current environment and its requirements? Sales forces need to have the power to fire their Sales Support if there isn't any true benefit. If Sales Support is not found effective in supporting sales, then the money spent on this endeavor can be better utilized on additional resources to make sure the *sales professionals* do not have to be involved in the **Fulfillment** or **Support stages** and to help with acquiring more qualified leads.

Sales Support should provide tools for the sales force, such as white papers, references / letters of recommendation, email, letters, proposal templates, competitive analysis, sales equipment support for the PC's, PDA's, etc.

Ultimate Fulfillment and Support Strategy for Any Company

If you are in upper management and can make significant changes in the company, by either understanding that there is a need to take full responsibility or just to make a good thing better, you will be making the single most valuable step that will have the largest impact on increasing your company's sales.

Can you handle the truth? As I mentioned at the beginning of the book, Chris Kent, an expert in Jeet Kune Do, warned me to be careful to offer reality to most people in small doses. Certainly, too many *Truths* offered all at once will be difficult to digest. For those companies that follow the steps I have laid out here, your sales force will see a dramatic rise in sales. Let's examine these concepts.

Culture of Caring about More Business and the Customer's Success

The company has to have a *Culture of Caring* about getting more business and truly caring about your customers' success. This kind of thinking is very common among *sales professionals*; it is hardwired. "Everyone in the company is in Sales" and everyone needs to think like a *sales professional*, from the top down. To have a culture of caring, this has to be a top goal of any company.

> **KEY TAKEAWAY**
>
> **Every employee has to think like a Sales Professional and care about the success of his or her customers.**

Sales professionals create employment for their co-workers. As part of a *Culture of Caring* and thinking like *sales professionals,* top management needs to educate all employees that *sales professionals* create more job security, raises, perks and benefits. Co-workers should understand that a good *sales professional* is a *revenue-generating* machine.

When I first started working for Mark Clark, the *Culture of Caring* was the best of any company I have ever worked at. I have had co-workers thank me for both new and existing business. Such appreciation motivated me to work even harder to sell more, which would help secure all our jobs, raises and benefits.

> **KEY TAKEAWAY**
>
> **Good Sales Professionals not only create more employment, they create more job security.**

To foster a *Culture of Caring,* top management has to train everyone from the top down to have a sales mentality. The catchphrase: "It isn't what you say but HOW you say it" should be placed on signs all over the company, so whoever comes in contact with customers will be reminded of the company's need for an excellent image and the customer's need for confidence in the company.

Teach avoidance of "We don't do it that way" and suggest "Is there another way we could accomplish the same thing?" The examples are endless, but successful company images begin with training.

It is important to place your customers into A, B, C, D and E categories. This is usually based on total profitability or the total cost of doing business with that customer. This is also a useful tool to determine how much support you are going to give a particular client. B2C examples may help to understand how many companies reward their most profitable customers. Some examples are:

(1) In the airline industry, if you are a preferred customer, you receive first class seating and you get little perks other passengers do not receive. As frequent flyers you acquire additional rewards.

(2)   Many businesses offer free shipping if the order meets a minimum amount. The same is true in determining the level of support your company is going to give a particular customer. Just make sure it is the company providing this additional support and not your sales force. They are focusing on more job security, which is a code word for *revenue-generating activities.*

Customer Support and Sales Support

Customer Support should handle all questions about existing orders, pricing, deliver dates, invoicing, back orders, etc. This structuring allows outside *sales professionals* to go outside and sell. "Everyone is in sales", but some people are better at dealing directly with your customers. Make sure that the employees helping the customer with their support questions or problems are knowledgeable and friendly. This employee should be someone a *sales professional* would pick to be a main contact. Do not make your sales force mentally or physically distracted with doing *damage control* and *babysitting.*

Good Customer Support can be vital to a *sales professional's* success. They can provide critical *Intelligence* on current and prospective customers, and they can continually take your most lucrative customer's "pulse". It is crucial to know whether they are unhappy or ecstatic with your company's products and services.

I have had co-workers help me avoid problems by giving me a heads up that a particular customer didn't sound too happy. Also, I have had co-workers pass on great sales leads. They were actually passing on problems a customer was having, and this gave me an opportunity to offer solutions and make more sales. With a sales mentality, we are all always looking for new sales opportunities and caring about the customer's success.

Sales Support should be just what the name says it is, support for sales. Depending on the size of the company, Customer Support and Sales Support could be one department. If it is combined, then it needs to be focused on supporting the needs of your customers *and* your sales force. If a customer complains, a company usually listens and tries to make things right. Sales Support needs to look at the sales force and the *sales professional* as their *internal customers.*

- What do *sales professionals* need to be successful?
- Sales reporting processes that are automated.
- Laptops, cellular phones and PDAs.

- Testimonials that are accessible, easy to find and obtain.
- Additional sales material that is up to date and accessible.

Many Sales Support functions that are beneficial are administrative and/or secretarial. This is busy work that needs to be done, but not by a highly paid *sales professional.* Sales Support could be providing Subject Experts for sales calls. Subject Experts are becoming more important than ever for closing new business.

Any Subject Expert's relationship with a *sales professional* should be like the martial arts Yin and Yang. This symbol became famous by the late, great Bruce Lee. As I understand it, this was a Chinese symbol to represent that it takes two halves to make a whole, not necessarily opposites but complementary to one and other. Nowadays I prefer to say *synergy*, when combined the sum is greater than the total of the two halves. When working together, the benefit becomes greater than the two working separately.

Yin and Yang

The best way to know how Sales Support truly can aid the sales force is to ask the sales force what they need most. Does the sales force need help with good leads, evaluating and qualifying incoming sales inquiries and/or competitive information? A company's goal should be to make sure that if their sales force were asked to evaluate the Customer Service and Sales Support, the sales force would say that both are vital to their success.

Companies need to look at the **Strategic Selling Cycle** and at the **Fulfillment & Support Strategy stages** to determine who in the company will be responsible and accountable. This will allow the *sales professionals* to be active in the other *revenue-generating* stages of the cycle.

So, just as my former boss, Mark Clark said, "The steps are not that complicated. The tough part is consistently executing the steps day after day."

Proper handling of the **Fulfillment & Support Strategy stages** is one of the most important things a company can do to help a sales force increase their sales. Can your company handle the truth?

KEY TAKEAWAY

Don't let what you can't do interfere with what you can do.

John Wooden, Basketball Hall of Famer

8

Expanding Strategy Stage

Land and Expand

Lily Pad "Threaded"

Continued Customer Education

By now, I hope everyone has an understanding about the importance of *sales professionals* doing *RGAs – revenue-generating activities*. One of the main ways to accomplish this goal is by having *sales professionals* spend more of their time in the retention, qualifying, prospecting, closing and the expanding stages of the **Strategic Selling Cycle**. I have had tremendous success spending time in the **Retention stage** and then using the **Expanding stage** for prospecting existing customers. Once you have landed a customer, it should be an on-going process to gain the largest share of their wallet. I call it "Land and Expand." But remember, it is difficult to land if you haven't even taken off yet because you are being grounded at the **Fulfillment & Support stages**.

Many of the previous **SSC** stages strategies, ideas and techniques can be *threaded* and *connected* into the **Expanding Strategy stage**. Remember the power of *threading* proven strategies, techniques and ideas, once they have been proven highly effective. *Threading* proven, field tested strategies and techniques will save you time and make you money.

The **Expanding Strategy stage** can and will overlap with the other stages. In the MMA world, the Contact Manipulation range was and still is being overlooked by many. But as the sport has evolved, it now is a stage that requires study and mastery to be successful in today's competitive environment. The **Expanding Strategy stage** is a range and/or stage in sales that has been one of the most important keys to my success. Studies have shown that many companies are not happy with the up-selling and cross-selling abilities of their sales forces. In a large survey, it was found that nearly a third of the companies' sales executives rated their sales forces as "poor" at both up-selling and cross-selling. However, the main reason for the sales executives' dissatisfaction is due to their companies' lack of training for their sales forces in the **Expanding Strategy stage**. Most companies spend 90 percent of their focus on prospecting for new customers, not prospecting their existing ones.

The **Expanding Strategy stage** completes one rotation of the **Strategic Selling Cycle**, which is a never-ending group of phases to help facilitate continued sales growth. The end of the **SSC** is just the beginning of the next cycle.

The **Expanding stage** is where you focus on gaining more business and a larger market share from your existing customers. The **Retention stage** is where the focus is on keeping and retaining the customers you have. Yes, there is overlap, but these stages have to be looked at, analyzed, studied and utilized separately in order to achieve maximum benefit.

Existing Accounts/Customers

I have heard often that the close of a sale is not the end but the beginning of a new relationship. This is a mindset that needs to be taught to everyone in a company, especially sales managers and sales forces. Companies need to train and educate all employees to be constantly looking for new opportunities to support their existing customers.

Having the **Expanding Strategy stage** as part of a company's

> **KEY TAKEAWAY**
> **Closing your first order can be the beginning of a long-term relationship and long-term prospecting opportunity.**

sales cycle helps educate, train and focus a company's employees and sales force to be experts at constantly looking for new opportunities to help existing customers. Yes, all employees should be trained to recognize opportunities with existing customers. The degree of training will vary, but it is important that all employees understand always to be on the lookout for new opportunities to help out existing customers. Then, they should pass on that information or *intelligence* to the sales force to *follow up* on.

Existing customers are goldmines ready to be dug out by a company's sales force. I have read some articles by sales experts using the same word, goldmine, but I want to take it a step further. Remember the 80-20 Rule. 80 percent of your business comes from 20 percent of your customers. Therefore, companies need to look at their existing goldmines as having many years of reserves left, but that valuable gold can only be brought out if continued, diligent mining is practiced. This is a mindset that companies, sales managers and their sales forces need to embrace.

For most existing customers, you have already done the hard part. You have gotten the order(s) and gained their trust. Now is the opportunity to use that *leverage* to gain more business with a lot less effort.

As mentioned in the **Prospecting Strategy stage**, the first place to start looking for more business is with the company's existing customers. As study after study has shown, existing customers are substantially easier to sell to, so why would anyone want to start anywhere else? Many sales experts agree. Tom Hopkins says that the most overlooked method for finding new business is when you prospect your own client base. This seems to be another *Universal Truth*.

KEY TAKEAWAY

Existing customers are goldmines ready to be dug out by a company's sales force!

As mentioned in the **Retention stage**, good existing accounts are like "Fort Knox", they need guards. Many companies make the mistake of not wanting to give any existing accounts away to *sales professionals*. The company feels that a *sales professional* would be unfairly compensated by not having to earn the business. Additionally, another classic mistake is when the company believes that since they have had the customer's business for years, this business is secure. There are two main reasons why a company needs to assign a *sales professional* as "Guard". (1) To protect the account from competitors and (2) To be looking continually for new opportunities to increase the wallet share.

In today's ultra-competitive environment, your competitor's ultimate goal is to take the customer from you. Most of the time, companies with "house accounts" would be much better off by having a *sales professional* get inside the existing account to search for other opportunities.

At Kinko's, I used the **Expanding Strategy** to obtain more and new business. Over and over again I would investigate smaller accounts to determine the customer's true potential. I grew many small accounts, categorized as a *D* account, into good *C* and *B* accounts. One such customer ended up growing into an *A* account.

To grow this small customer into an A account, I called a key contact there and used my "*Just want to you give a quick update*" technique. Remember, this technique is part of my *CCE - Continued Customer Education* strategy. I ended up talking with one of the owners and he came by one of our branches so we could meet. After our short meeting, I gave him my quick update and he told me he was totally unaware of all our capabilities. He said he was thankful he talked to me, because he was starting to look towards other vendors. Since he did not think we could continue to handle the larger and larger runs of his manuals, he was about to start searching for a supplier. Wow! What a perfect case study of why it is continually important to educate your customers.

The *CCE - Continued Customer Education* strategy is the umbrella under which I have used many techniques to drastically increase a current customer's business.

CCE - Continued Customer Education

As has been a theme throughout several stages of the **SSC**, education is a key to continued success with your customers. Many occupations require continued education, CXE, for renewal of their professional licenses. Doctors are required to get CME - Continued Medical Education or an attorney, CLE - Continued Legal Education. Companies have to provide continuing education that helps their customers succeed in business. The education, *CCE - Continued Customer Education,* can be on how your company's latest products and services will aid in the customer company's success.

I challenge companies to survey their existing customer base. See how knowledgeable your customers are about all your current products and services. From my experience, most companies will be shocked by the results. Most companies' existing customers do not have a clue about all the products and services your company offers.

As part of the *"Just want to give you a quick update"* technique I used at Kinko's, I would tell my customer that many times I have been told, " I was in your branch picking up a personal order and noticed a product being produced and ask when did you start having the capability to make those?" The answer they were often given was, "For a couple of years." Now, that is <u>not</u> the best way to market your new products and services. Then, I would go into my what's new the last two years at Kinko's routine for ten minutes. As discussed in the **Closing Strategy stage**, I would go through a coupon book with some samples and often would get a response similar to, "We have been looking to find someone who is capable of helping us with that."

The above opportunity was created by using my *CCE - Continued Customer Education* strategy, which created a prospect in the **Expanding stage**. I also "Lowered the risk to buy" with the coupons and the fact that I have proven my company and myself by having a proven track record.

> **BIG MISTAKE**
> **Most existing customers DO NOT know about all the products and services your company offers.**

As mentioned in the **Prospecting Strategy stage**, putting on seminars, webinars and site tours are excellent ways to help you and your company provide valuable *CCE - Continued Customer Education.* As a reminder, try to make sure the emphasis is on education and not sales. Customers will thank you for your continued focus on CCE by buying more, so be careful not to structure your CCE as a sales pitch in disguise.

Using my *"Just want to give you a quick update"* technique in the **Expanding stage** is another perfect way to continually educate your existing customers on what's new as well as old services they were unaware of. Your customers' time is valuable, so make sure you stress education as a way to help the customer improve their business. A small token of appreciation does not hurt either: coupons for future orders, inexpensive giveaways, pens, coffee cups etc.

The idea that I talked about in **Closing Strategy stage**: "Never Decide for the Customer" is also tied into the CCE. By continually educating your customer on what products and services you offer, you will be surprised how they find a need or benefit that you didn't know about. As a *sales professional,* you have to be careful about thinking that you know what products and services your customer needs. Briefly telling customers about all of your products and services may cause them to see a benefit to their business that you were not aware of. Accordingly, you can tie your company's products and services into improving their business.

The best opportunity for crossing-selling and up-selling is in the **Expanding Strategy stage**. Many additional sales are easy when cross-selling and/or up-selling; once the customer knows all of the items your company has to offer them. The *sales professional* is educating the customer in the other products and services the company offers when cross-selling or is educating on the benefits on buying the next level up of products or services when up-selling. Again, you are always trying to gain a larger portion of the customer's wallet.

Now, I will finish my story from the **Prospecting Strategy stage** on how my branch won the Inland Northwest District award for Kinko's commercial sales force. It was a Christmas and holiday promotions sales contest. We were competing against branches in all of Idaho, Montana, parts of Washington and Oregon. (Quick reminder: top sales management had a teleconference for all the branches to let everyone know there was an upcoming contest and for the branch that sold the most Christmas and holiday promotional items, management at that branch would get a cash prize.) Some examples of items to be sold were personalized calendars, tree ornaments and stationary. This was a collection of retail items, and they wanted the outside sales force to do cold calls and to sell the promotional items to existing customers.

> **BIG MISTAKES**
>
> **Not remembering to do the numbers**
>
> **Not remembering the difference between B2C and B2B**

I did the numbers and it was impossible for me to sell enough of the promotional items for me to make my monthly quota. Plus, the opportunity cost of focusing on the Christmas holiday items would prevent me from making my monthly quota. Having a B2B *sales professional* sell retail items to one consumer at a time is a BIG MISTAKE. I understood the difference between selling retail and selling large volume, which is typical for B2B sales, so I didn't do one cold call. However, I did sell one of the largest single holiday orders. It was personalized holiday cards for the President and CEO of one of my largest customers. It was a $284 order, but I wanted to show my face in the executive office and to "babysit" the order to guarantee that nothing went wrong with it. I did not have total faith in our **Fulfillment & Support stages**.

Well what *did* I do? Each branch would receive a box of nice holiday colored brochures giving an overview of all the holiday items. Additionally, they would send each branch a bunch of 25-percent-off holiday coupons. I was told that many times most of the brochures and coupons would end up being thrown away. I took lots of both, and at the end of every meeting I had with new prospective customers, I would have a *talk off*, "Oh, by the way, here is a brochure with all the new holiday items. My parents' favorite Santa Clause gift every year is a personalized calendar with my family photos. With this coupon, it is under $20." I would hand these out to everyone, and if anyone had questions, I would recommend that they call or go into the branch for costs and timelines. I also did the same thing by dropping by existing customers, where I touched bases and used the same *talk off*.

I was focusing on the **Expanding Strategy stage** and I was creatively cross-selling. All the customers loved me for giving them inexpensive holiday gift ideas at a discount. Knowing that our inside *sales professional* was totally dependable and knowledgeable, I felt comfortable suggesting that they call her with any questions.

Our inside *sales professional* told me that she had to set up a table by the front entrance because so many people were coming in to buy holiday promotional items. She told me that numerous customers placed large orders and mentioned the coupons I had given them. Surprisingly, the top sales management never asked our branch manager or me what we did to win the contest over all the other branches in four states.

During that time period, I was the only Territory Sales Representative to not only make goal, but I also exceeded it four months in a row. Again, I never received a call on what was I doing. However, I did get a few "good job, again" comments when the Regional Operations manager was in town. Unfortunately, neither she nor anyone else ever went the next step and asked, "What are you doing?"

As always, I was following the *MSA methodology.* I drove in the business NOT by working harder but by working smarter.

As I mentioned in the **Closing Strategy stage**, up-selling is another technique of trying to gain a large portion of the customer's wallet by selling the better or enhanced and more expensive version, which can yield a higher value solution of the product or service. The examples varied by company, but one example is when I worked for Simplex in the Service Division. An existing customer with a "testing only" agreement for their fire alarm would call in for a service call. This would be a perfect time for me to revisit with them the importance of an agreement that covers equipment too, thus avoiding the unexpected expense of equipment failure. I would up-sell from the mandatory annual testing to also include panel coverage and, in some cases, coverage for the panel plus all peripheral devices, i.e., smoke and heat detectors, pull stations, etc.

Another example is when I worked for Trend/West Coast. I would always try to sell the displays of all new products. I would stress the customer's starting a new product's sales off with a "bang" from the additional exposure of a display. Accordingly, I would try to sell the customer on bringing in a new product and buying the display that showed it off to best advantage. Additionally, I often did the same thing when I worked at Warner Lambert. When a new product would come out, it was the company's goal to have me place the new product and also sell a supporting display. Cross-selling and up-selling were always easier techniques to use on existing customers because I already have their trust. Remember that creative *bundling* of your products and services can help you automatically up-sell and/or cross-sell.

Lily Pad technique... Threaded

One of the best ways to understand the **Expanding Strategy stage** is by using my *lily pad* analogy, as I previously discussed in the **Prospecting Strategy stage**. Remember to imagine a frog jumping from lily pad to lily pad. Now imagine your *sales professional* jumping from the Human Resource department to the Marketing department. Once establishing business relationships with those two departments, jumping from department to department is an excellent and efficient way to prospect.

This is one of my favorite techniques, I have used it numerous times in my sales career and I continue to do so to this day. An example is when I worked at Kinko's and I had a great relationship with the HR department at a local hospital. I strategically decided to drop off an order that we had rushed to complete in order to help them out of a bind. My HR contact thanked me for being her life saver once again, and I thanked her for their continued business. I then asked her who would be the best person in the marketing department to introduce myself to. She told me to come with her, she proceeded to walk me down the hall to the director of marketing and she introduced me as "Human Resource's life saver". Wow! The director of marketing asked me to come in and explain our services. I had used my relationship with the human resources department as *leverage* and performed the *lily pad* technique to jump to the next department and next opportunity.

Remember to *thread* strategies, ideas and techniques in as many places as possible so you don't have to keep relearning the new ideas and techniques. Once you find a *high percentage technique*, just as I do in my martial arts training, try to find as many places as possible to utilize it against your competition.

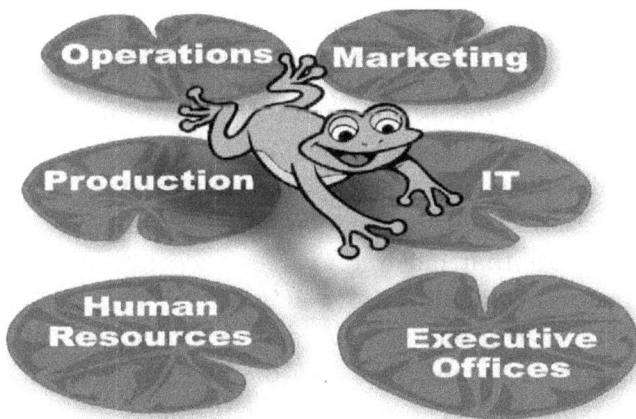

Lily Pad Technique

Remember that there are many great ideas and techniques that are *Truths* and *Universal Truths*. I have used the saying "Land and Expand" for years, but I heard it again several times when reading some of the Gartner Group's research. It is a great saying to reinforce the **Expanding Strategy stage**. Focusing on expanding business with an existing customer is a *Universal Truth* for gaining new sales. Companies and sales forces always need to be on the lookout for new ways to gain a greater share of their existing clients' budgets. Once you secure a new customer, then you want to expand into as many departments of a company as you can.

Volume Discounting Technique

When I worked at Kinko's, I would track my customers' volume of business. When meeting with customers, I showed them the volume of business they were giving us and explained that if they increased their business by not that much more on a monthly basis they would often be able to qualify for the next level of volume discounting. I would also go into my *CCE - Customer Continued Education* strategy by explaining our other products and services that would help them reach the next level. Many times the customer would increase their purchasing a little each month. By doing this monthly over a year's time, it would add up to a nice increase of additional business. This would be a win-win for the customer, Kinko's and me because the total business would really add up. I used this technique repeatedly to expand many customers' total purchases with small monthly increases.

Hunters and Farmers

There are many types of personalities, each having strengths and weaknesses. Some *sales professionals* are better at "hunting", going out and getting new business, while other *sales professionals* have better natural skill sets at "farming", building existing relationships.

By finding and securing new business, hunters are the type of *sales professionals* that most companies associate with good *selling* traits. There are personality traits that give an advantage to certain types of activities. Hunters are the models companies are looking for in their *sales professionals*, because they usually have high energy, are aggressive and exhibit never give-up attitudes. Hunters are great at prospecting.

On the other hand, farmers are the ones who historically help maintain and cultivate relationships with existing clients. They do not always have the same traits as a hunter. They are often the ones put in the role to be the account manager of a good customer. Farmers are great at the **Retention stage**.

I have worked for companies that have official account managers of their big accounts, and I have witnessed some great people with the

186

ability to maintain and build relationships with their big customers who can be very demanding. All large accounts need an account manager for the best chance of retaining the customer. Companies should understand that managing these large accounts can take a lot of time and effort. Many times, they turn into a full time job for the *sales professional.*

Few companies have the luxury of employing both types of personalities with designations as *sales professionals* who <u>*only*</u> prospect for new business or who <u>*only*</u> handle existing accounts. Consequently, hunters need to be trained to become better farmers and farmers have to learn to develop some hunting traits.

Expanding Strategy Stage... Helps Keep the Competition Out!

Companies and their sales forces that follow the **Expanding Strategy** help keep the competition out of existing accounts and away from customers. This is accomplished in several ways. Continually educating customers builds trust and expands your sales force's ability to cross-sell and up-sell, which will increase the depth of customer/ account penetration of your products and services. All this attention lessens the likelihood that customers will feel the need to look for other vendors to improve their business. This leads to fewer opportunities for the competition to get their foot in the customer's door.

KEY TAKEAWAY

Remember, <u>existing</u> customers can be a goldmine, so dig!

9

Final Thoughts

Theories never made a sale

Bring more science to the art

Remember my personal motto in life and in sales: "Working harder at working smarter". This applies to every company, sales manager and *sales professional.* If I had found someone to teach me a realistic *base* and a proven sales methodology, then I would have saved years of experimenting. Now others can benefit from my hard work and mistakes to improve their sales skills with speed and efficiency.

Over the years, I have been in numerous sales training classes and found that much, if not most of what was being taught was too far from the reality of the real world of "in the trenches" sales. In his eBook, *Back to the Basics of Selling,* Gerhard Gschwandtner makes a great point: "Theories never made a sale." For too many years, the martial arts world accepted unproven theories as *The Truth.* Finally, the UFC proved that the majority of these theories never magically protected anyone.

Companies need a formal sales methodology, such as the MSA - mixed selling arts, that everyone even remotely involved in sales is trained on, which is reinforced from top management down and utilizes a common language. A strong, proven *base,* such as the **Strategic**

Selling Cycle, managed by a Customer Relationship Management system is sure to improve sales. Following a process and utilizing a CRM system will "bring more science to the art of selling."

A Culture of Learning that stresses the need for continually refining and improving sales strategies and methods will *increase your odds* of producing more sales. Developing an ingrained mentality that promotes constant refinements and adjustments is part of the game and part of the fun.

My success has come from following the *MSA methodology*, which was and is being built on *Truths* and *Universal Truths*. You and your company need to do the same. Don't just accept what I say, but take a look at recent studies which report that 90 percent of companies that follow a structured sales methodology say they have had improved performance, code word for more sales!

KEY TAKEAWAY

B2B sales is an art. However, the key is to bring more science to the art.

The following ACTIONS make for successful sales: **Retain** customers, **Qualify** for profitable opportunities, **Prospect** for new business, **Close** new business and look for ways to continually **Expand** your business with existing customers. It is equally important that companies take full responsibility for **Fulfillment & Support**, once products and services are sold.

I have provided examples of numerous strategies and techniques that were proven in the field, but there are others that are yet to be uncovered. Stick with the basics and you will be successful, even if others in your company "Can't handle the truth!" The *Universal Truths* covered here represent the keys to successful sales for any company today. Remember, success comes not from *complicated moves* but from *sophisticated basics*!

I have mentioned that a great attitude is crucial for the success of any company, sales manager or *sales professional*, but the key is to combine a great attitude with ACTION. ACT by following a proven sales system backed with an overall methodology. Then, you will reap the greatest potential.

Adopt what you find useful in this book. The ideas, techniques and strategies presented here have been and still are being used successfully today. They are *NOT* theories and many *WILL increase your odds* of more sales.

H.W. Shaw once said, "The greatest thief this world had ever produced is procrastination and he's still at large."

Don't just finish this book and think about it. Start to **apply** the ideas today!

As your referee and coach, listen to my instructions: keep your chin up, let's see a great attitude and now... ACTION!

GLOSSARY

80/20 Rule – This is a Universal Truth in the sales world and almost every other aspect of life. Twenty percent of your efforts will result in eighty percent of the results. For example, eighty percent of your profitable sales will come from twenty percent of your customers.

Advanced Basics – Continual refinement and improvement of the Basics. This term is also used by the great American Brazilian Jiu-Jitsu, MMA fighter, B.J. Penn. Interchangeable with sophisticated basics.

Attitude – A general feeling about something. Having a great attitude is one of the main keys for any company, sales manager or sales professional's success. Attitude is like physical fitness, it needs to be constantly worked on to maintain and improve.

Approach – Thinking and planning before the first attempt at personal interaction between you and the prospect. Approach is the action before meeting with a prospect for the first time. (See Set Up)
Most of the time, you are trying to gain *intelligence* and make the first personal contact a warm call.

Aware – Having knowledge from having made an observation. In the martial arts world, being aware is a key part of self-defense. The same is true in the selling arts world. Companies and *sales professionals* have to be constantly aware of changes in the environment, especially changes to customer situations.

B2B (business-to-business) – Interactions between a business and another business. Whether prospecting or closing, you are trying to gain business from another company, not a private individual.

B2C (business-to-consumer) – Interactions between a business and an individual. Any time you, as a private individual, go into a store to buy something for yourself or another person, it is a B2C.

Babysitting – A term used when a company continually fails in the fulfillment and support stages and the sales professional has to get involved in order to ensure the customer gets what was promised.

Basics – The fundamental building blocks of any endeavor. In sales, examples of basics would be retention, qualifying, prospecting, closing and expanding business.

Base – The core moves and strategies around which a company or sales professional builds everything else. SSC - Strategic Selling Cycle is an example of a base for a successful sales process.

Big Mistake – A saying used by Brazilian Jiu-Jitsu expert Pedro Carvalho in his training series. He let the viewers know that doing a particular move at a particular time would have a high probability of failure. Also, a comment to inform readers that particular sales ideas and strategies have a high probability of failure.

Bundling – The act of combining products and services. A company tries to increase the size of the purchase by offering several products or services together at a lower price, hoping to persuade the buyer to choose the package deal vs. buying just one of the items.

Bone Burier – An analogy of a dog burying all his bones without taking time to savor them and forgetting where he has buried them when they are needed. Collecting strategies, ideas and techniques but applying them in a realistic environment. The difference between memorizing and internalizing.

CCE (Continued Customer Education) – A focus by the sales force and their company on continually updating and educating their customers on how to be more successful. Passing on best practices in combination with utilizing your company's products and services.

Change in Guard – When a key contact has left the position, either left the company or changed positions within his company. Every time a key contact in a customer changes, it is critical you have a plan of action a strategy to introduce and sell yourself and your company to the new contact.

Complicated Moves – Mistake made by many to make strategies and techniques so complex that they start to lose their usability in a realistic environment. Mario Sperry, MMA and Brazilian Jiu-Jitsu former champion and expert instructor says complicated moves are the ones you see on training videos but never in competition.

Connected – Mario Sperry, MMA and Brazilian Jiu-Jitsu former champion and expert instructor, said, "All the moves and techniques I show you are all connected." This is a very important point to be successful at sales. Strategies, ideas and techniques are used in combination in many areas and are all connected. Ideas will be utilized again in combination, to build and enhance each other in many areas of the SSC - Strategic Selling Cycle.

Core Moves – The time tested basic actions in the sales world. They are retention, qualifying, prospecting closing and expanding to name a few. They are the foundation that everything else is continually built around.

Cost of Acquisition – The total cost to a business for acquiring a new customer. If taken into consideration, the business might find that they cannot afford the new customer.

CRM (Customer Relationship Management) – A software based tool to track the interactions between a business and its customers and prospects. Historically, it has been used mainly as a tracking and reporting tool of sales forces' activities for management. Many sales forces use it as an expensive, mandated and automated contact address book. When used correctly, it is the ultimate sales tool, because it can help companies, sales managers and sales forces to be more process-dependent and increase sales.

Cross-Selling – A technique used to try to convince a customer to buy similar items in a product line or service. Examples are to carry more sizes or an additional line of a product.

CSE (Continued Sales Education) – The goal of any sales force or sales professional should be to continue to learn and improve their skills. Sales professionals should strive to keep learning as an integral part of their professional development. The key is to learn and then apply.

Culture of Caring – Companies have to have a culture of caring to get more business and to enhance their customers' ability to succeed. This type of thinking is very common among sales professionals.

CXO – Now a common term used, because there are becoming so many variations of the term Chief Officer: CEO - chief executive officer, CFO - chief financial officer, COO - chief operations officer and CSO - chief sales officer, to name a few.

Damage Control – A slang term used when a sales professional gets involved in the Fulfillment and Support stages of the Strategic Selling Cycle after a coworker has said or done something to anger the customer. The sales professional intervenes to repair any damage to the business relationship.

Dormant Account – An account that once did business with your company but now has not reordered or done business for a specific amount of time.

Environment – Senior Grandmaster Ed Parker said that the environment is the #1 consideration in a self-defense situation. He stated that the environment is what is <u>in you</u>, <u>on you</u> and <u>around you</u>. One of the top considerations in sales is to adapt and adjust strategies and techniques as the environment changes.

Equation Formula – An idea created by Senior Grand Master Ed Parker. To any given base, you can prefix, suffix, insert, rearrange, alter, adjust, regulate and delete ideas and moves. This concept applies in the MSA - *mixed selling arts* world. The sales professional has a base but will always have alternatives as the situation changes.

Farmers – Sales professionals who help maintain relationships with existing clients. Although not always having the same traits as hunters, they are the ones put in the role to be the account manager of a good customer. Farmers excel at the Retention Strategy stage.

Follow Up – Just as in mixed martial arts (MMA) competitions; throwing one technique followed by another technique substantially increases the chance of damage and success. This is applicable to *mixed selling arts*; good follow up is the key to more sales. The specifics of follow up are called next steps.

Forward Momentum – One of the main keys to successful sales is to try to always keep opportunities moving forward toward the close. Forward momentum is a larger generalized principle of follow up and next steps.

Framework – An organized structure for the sales force and or sales department. MSA framework it is represented by a triangle with language/terminology on the right side, CRM on the bottom and CSE on the left side. The SSC (Strategic Selling Cycle) is inside the triangle and Attitude with Action is in the middle.

Gatekeeper – A term used for the people in a company who help screen out unwanted solicitations. Many times they keep sales professionals from the decision makers.

Good, Better, Best – A sales technique in which the goal is to narrow down the options to the three best choices for a customer. This helps speed up the customer's decision making and aids the sales professional in closing more sales.

High Percentage Moves/Techniques – Moves or techniques that have a high probability of success. They have been tested in a realistic environment.

House Account – A customer that a company has determined to be super-loyal or a secure customer. Such customer accounts need great account managers, i.e., sales professionals.

Hunters – The type of sales professionals that most companies consider having the best selling traits. They find and secure new business, are high energy, aggressive and never give up. These traits give them an advantage for success in certain types of activities. Hunters do extremely well at the Prospecting and Closing Strategy stages.

Increase your odds – Whether in sales or the martial arts world, one of the main goals is to constantly try to increase the odds for success. One should always strive to improve by utilizing high percentage moves and/or strategies to increase the probability of success.

Intelligence – Specific information about a customer and its key contacts that will help a business obtain, retain, maintain and grow more sales. An example would be knowing that a prospect is unsatisfied with their current vendor.

Internal Customers – Fellow employees or coworkers are vital to any sales professional's success. Treat each like a customer with respect and a thank you, so they continue to act as loyal customers who aid in sales success.

Just want to give you a quick update – A technique I have used successfully for years to get an appointment. I tell the prospect that I want to give them some valuable information that would be beneficial to help them in their business in the future. Then, they would know who could help them out when the need arose. I would also toss in some coupons and/or incentives for their time.

Leverage – To increase your advantage and minimize your opponent's efforts is one of the main goals of Brazilian Jiu-Jitsu. The same is true in the sales world. Companies and sales professionals constantly must try to increase their leverage and decrease their competitor's.

Lily Padding – An analogy of thinking about how a frog jumps from lily pad to lily pad. In prospecting, I use this technique when I am visiting with a prospect or an existing customer. I am always looking around for other prospects on the same floor, building, building next door, down the street and on the way to the appointment. Then, just like a frog jumping from lily pad to lily pad, I jump from prospect to prospect.

Low Percentage Moves – Moves or techniques that have a low probability of success. Techniques that might work well in theory or in untested situations but have a high failure rate in a realistic environment.

Lower Cost of Ownership – All the costs of owning a product and/or service taken into consideration, not just the upfront cost but the total cost over time. With all costs taken into consideration, your offer is a lower cost than the competitor's option.

MSA Methodology, mixed selling arts – A field of continual study of sales methods built around a base of Universal Truths. Striving constantly to improve and sophisticate the basics. Ultimately, it is a way of making learning and improving a way of life. It includes sales terminology, sales automation and continued sales education.

MSA model, mixed selling arts – A sales model created by observing the mixed martial arts revolution. It has become a sales methodology where the base and framework are built around Universal Truths. Continually searching for new refinements to constantly improve. Making learning and improving a way of life.

MMA model, mixed martial arts – Looking at the martial arts world with the revolution that started with the UFC (Ultimate Fighting Championships) and using it as a model for continued improvement. Now the competitions are called the mixed martial arts, because they comprise all the ranges of competitive fighting. All fighters' appear similar, because Universal Truths were discovered at each range of fighting.

Next Steps – A sub-category of forward momentum and a major key to the success of any sales professional. Just as in chess, you are always thinking of the next move or moves. Next steps are the specifics of your follow up.

Order Starter – A small order you try to get from a prospect, so they will give you and your company a chance to show the high level of service you can provide. A small order would be a lower risk to try you and your company out. It helps you get your "foot in the door."

Post-Call review – After meeting with a prospect, sales professionals need to review how the meeting went. What could they have said differently or better?

Pre-Call review – Before each meeting, sales professionals need to review the agenda. What are they going to say and stress in the meeting? Is there any intelligence that can be used to strengthen your company's offering?

Project – A product or service that is usually a one-time transaction.

It does not have a high probability of repeat business. One example would be printing a grand opening banner for a new business.

Program – A product or service that is used on a repeat basis. An example would be printing of a monthly newsletter for an organization.

Promise – The product and/or service the sales professional and company have agreed to provide to a customer for a certain price.

Reduce the Risk – A strategy to try to reduce the risk of making a change. With change, there is always a risk. You have to reduce the risk and then make the problem the customer has appear to be significant enough that it is a risk not to take action with you.

Revenue-Generating Activities, **RGAs** – Activities that focus the sales professional's time on bringing in revenue and profit. Ensuring that most of the sales professional's time is focused on retention, prospecting and closings would be considered a key. Having the sales professional focus too much on fulfillment, support and administrative paperwork would be a waste of his/her talents.

Sales Professional – A title I use to refer to any person who has chosen a sales career. Sales is a profession and all salespeople should strive to be become professionals in their field.

Selling Arts – Just as the martial arts is historically known as the art of fighting, Selling Arts is the art of selling. Selling is an art and not a science.

Set Up – The key to successful prospecting and closing is not always the technique chosen but the set of preliminary steps taken before the techniques are put in motion. (See Approach)

Schmoozing – A term used in the sales world referring to chatting and giving incentives, lunches, game tickets, pens, calendars, giveaways and other free items to a customer to gain or reinforce a favorable relationship.

Sophisticated Basics – Continual refinement and improvement of the Basics. Interchangeable with Advanced Basics.

Specialized Moves – Moves in the martial arts that had a limited number of opportunities to be utilized successfully. In the mixed selling arts world, it might be sending a letter by using the postal service. Years ago, this tactic might have been effective, but in today's environment it has become less useful.

Spiel – A preplanned and thought out summary of the benefits of working with your company. An overview of the benefits to a company to use your company's products and services.

SSC (Strategic Selling Cycle) – A sales process that is comprised of the Universal Truths of selling. The cycle process includes a strategy framework for retention, qualifying, prospecting, closing, fulfillment, support and expanding business with prospects and customers.

Stirring Up The Dust – A saying that refers to creating an opportunity by making more cold calls, warm calls and follow-up calls.

Strategy – The art of carefully planning towards a specific goal to increase your chances of success.

Synergy – A term for the whole being greater than the sum of its parts. True teamwork can accomplish synergy.

Talk Offs/Talk Tracks – Talking points that have been thought out in advance. Often, they come about because the same types of questions are asked over and over by many different prospects and customers. You keep improving and refining until you sound well-spoken and knowledgeable about certain questions that are commonly asked by prospects and customers.

Target Audience – The potential customers who would be a fit (a profitable customer) for your company and the business which would benefit from your products and services. If a sales professional were limited to only 40 customers, would a certain prospect make the list, i.e., are they my target audience?

Technique – The method of accomplishing a desired result. Typically, pre-planned techniques have a better probability of success than random tactics and methods.

Threading/Threaded – Term to explain that once you have learned an idea, concept, technique or strategy and found it to be a Truth or Universal Truth, you apply it everywhere you can. This saves you time by not having to learn new things over and over again. Once it is proven, use it everywhere you can.

The Truth – The myth that particular ideas, concepts, techniques and/or strategies work for everyone in every situation. This is true only in a fantasy land. No human is the holder of The Truth. A term used by the late great martial artist Bruce Lee. Be it the MMA or the sales world, nobody is the holder of The Truth.

Third Point of View – One of Senior Grandmaster Ed Parker's ideas for gaining new perspective on an altercation. His idea was to learn from competitors, opponents and outside points of view. The amazing aspect of his idea is the new perspective acquired when you look from a bystander's point of view. There is a wealth of knowledge to be gained by taking a view from the outside looking in. The same is true in both the MMA and sales worlds.

Tool – Anything that will assist you to accomplish a specific task. Examples in sales could be a laptop, PDA, cellular phone, subject expert, letters of recommendation, testimonials, marketing material, etc.

Total Cost of Ownership – Taking into consideration the total cost of owning a product and/or service. Not just the upfront cost, but the total cost over time. (See Lower Cost of Ownership)

Touch Point – Anywhere a customer comes into contact with your company, especially with any human interactions. An employee talking with a customer would be an example.

Truth/Truths – Strategies, techniques and ideas that have worked under realistic conditions and have been found to have a high probability of success.

Turn a Cold Call into a Warm Call – A strategy for having credibility when you have done or are doing successful business with someone in the past or present. When making a first contact, they already have some reassurance or trust from someone you know. This is vital today with the amount of unrequested solicitations that many prospects receive on a daily basis. You do not want to make another blind solicitation.

Universal Truths – Strategies, techniques and ideas that have worked repeatedly under realistic conditions for numerous people and have been found to have a high probability of success over time.

Up-Selling – Another technique to gain a larger portion of the customer's budget. Many times, this is by selling a better or enhanced version of your product, service or solution, which is the more expensive version. A classic B2C example is "Would you like a large value meal?"

Warm Call – When making the first contact with a prospect, somehow they know of you or your company. It could be through a referral, reading an article, or any other way that makes the prospect favorably aware of you. In prospecting, it is always a goal to turn every cold call into a warm call. It lowers the risk of talking to you.

Yellow Card – In PRIDE Fighting Championship MMA events, a referee could give a Yellow Card for stalling if one or both of the fighters was not pressing the action. Three warnings will result in a disqualification.

REFERENCES

"Successful Selling in Turbulent Times - Dealing with an Economic Slowdown", *CSO Insights*, 2008, www.csoinsights.com

"Sales Performance Optimization: 2008 Survey Results and Analysis", *CSO Insights*, 2008

Sales Effectiveness - Pathways to Productivity, Alex Jefferies & Peter Ostrow, Aberdeen Group, 2008, www.aberdeen.com

"Sales 2.0 Whitepaper: Part 1 - Run Away to Join the New Circus" & "Part 2 - Think. Think Different. Think Again", *CSO Insights*, 2007

"Sales Effectiveness Best Practices Analysis Study", *CSO Insights*, 2007

"Target Marketing Priorities Analysis: 2007 Key Trends - B2B", *CSO Insights*, 2007

"The Impact of What You Say on Sales Performance, - Optimizing Sales Messaging", *CSO Insights*, 2007

Demand Generation, Kick-Start Your Business, Aberdeen Group, 2007

The New Science of Sales Force Productivity, Harvard Business Review, published September 2006

"Demystifying the Sales Effectiveness Challenge, What's Really Working, and How Often Are We Doing It", *CSO Insights*, "Key Challenges for CSOs in 2006", *CSO Insights*, 2006

"Sales Performance Optimization, 2006 Survey Results and Analysis", *CSO Insights*, 2006

"Sales Effectiveness Insights from the Executive Suite", *SIRIUS Decisions Research Brief*, 2006, www.siriusdecisions.com

"The Impact of Sales Process and CRM on Optimizing Sales Effectiveness - Summary Report (CSO Executive Briefing Series)", *CSO Insights*, 2005

Escaping The Price - Driven Sale: Selling to Clients at a Premium, Tom Snyder, Huthwaite, Inc., 2005, www.huthwaite.com

"Sales Effectiveness Insights - 2005 State of the Marketplace Review", *CSO Insights*, 2005

"Dynamic Sales Knowledge Management: What Sales Must Know to Win the Game", *CSO Insights*, 2005

Sales Effectiveness: It's about Collaboration, Aberdeen Group, 2004

Sales Effectiveness - Helping Sales Sell, Aberdeen Group, 2004

"Sales Effectiveness Insights: Optimizing Sales Performance with Consistent Message Management (CSO Executive White Paper Series)", *CSO Insights*, 2004

"Sales Effectiveness Insights, The Top Ten Trends for 2004, (CSO Executive White Paper Series)", *CSO Insights*, 2004

"Increasing Sales Effectiveness Through Optimized Sales Knowledge Management (CSO Executive White Paper Series)", *CSO Insights*, 2004

Back to the Basics of Selling, Gerhard Gschwandtner, Personal Selling Power (publisher), 2003, www.sellingpower.com

How Can Sales People Gain Access to Executives?, Gartner Study Group, Gartner Group, 2002
www.gartner.com

Selling to Big Companies and Multiple Ezine newsletters, Jill Konrath
www.SellingtoBigCompanies.com

Multiple Ezine newsletters, *Selling Power*, www.selling power. com

Multiple news columns, *Small Business Strategies*, Rhonda Abrams, www.PlanningShop.com

Multiple Ezine newsletters, *Dave Kahle & The DaCo Corporation*, www.davekahle.com

Multiple Ezine newsletters, Art Sobczak, *Business By Phone, Inc.*, www.businessbyphone.com

Multiple Ezine newsletters, Jeffrey Gitomer, *Buy Gitomer*, www. gitomer.com

Multiple Ezine newsletters, Robert Middleton, *Action Plan Marketing*, www.actionplan.com

Audio-Tech Business Book Summaries, numerous book summaries on CD's, topics on sales, marketing and business. www.audiotech.com

About the Author

Scott Marker is an Idaho native. He is a graduate of Boise State University with a degree in Business Administration. His first position out of college started him on his life-long study of business-to-business professional sales and he has spent 20 years doing "in the trenches" sales research. His on-the-job experience has shown that many sales ideas, techniques and strategies taught by leading companies make the same mistake that most martial arts schools make today, teaching unrealistic material for the real world.

This goal surpassing master of salesmanship has a black belt in the martial arts and in the selling arts. His straight talking, real world ideas have helped him become the Director of Marketing and Sales for two connected businesses and driven their sales to record levels in just four years.

Scott's sales background has been very diverse, having worked in seven different industries as an outside B2B (business-to-business) sales professional. Over the last 20 years, he has represented both small and Top100 companies. He worked for Warner Lambert, selling over-the-counter drugs and consumer health products; Moore Business Forms, the world's largest business forms producer at the time, as a developer of new accounts; Simplex, selling for both service and equipment divisions; Trend/WestCoast beauty products supplier; Kinko's, as a corporate account manager; Intermountain Technology Group as

the Microsoft® Solutions Specialist and also as a Security Solutions Specialist.

Scott Marker joined the Collection Bureau, Inc. and Account Billing Service in February of 2003. Scott's position gave him authority to run marketing and sales for both companies. This also gave him the opportunity and freedom to use what he had learned from his successful sales background to take the best concepts, strategies, ideas and techniques and put them to the test. He led the companies to record sales growth.

Mark Clark sold the Collection Bureau, Inc. and Account Billing Service at the end of 2008. Scott decided to move on and accepted a sales position with Bonneville Collections - Check Services.

This new challenge will once again allow Scott to follow his proven MSA Methodology, mixed selling arts.

> **"Remember, success is a journey, not a destination."**
> **Bruce Lee**

Please visit www.mixedsellingarts.com for information or questions on:

- **additional books**
- **speaking / seminars**
- **consulting**
- **general questions**

In addition, you can check out the authors B2B sales blog, which includes many real world sales strategies, techniques and ideas.